I'LL DIE LAUGHING!

I'll die laughing!

I'll Die Laughing!

by JOSEPH T. McGLOIN, S.J.

illustrated by DON BAUMGART

THE BRUCE PUBLISHING COMPANY
MILWAUKEE

271.5
M

IMPRIMI POTEST:

DANIEL H. CONWAY, S.J.
Provincial, Missouri Province

NIHIL OBSTAT:

JOHN A. SCHULIEN, S.T.D.
Censor librorum

IMPRIMATUR:

☩ ALBERT G. MEYER
Archiepiscopus Milwauchiensis

May 24, 1955

To

M. D. G.

Does a Jesuit hatch?

PREFACE

A FRIEND-BY-CORRESPONDENCE once asked me what the "S.J." behind my name meant. I told him, of course, that the letters stand for "Society of Jesus," and that you find them behind every Jesuit's name.

The thought then came to me that there must be a lot of people who do not know what "S.J." means, though their number is not nearly so great as the legion of those who are erroneously certain they know exactly what a Jesuit is.

I have, off and on, read things in which the word "Jesuitical" was used to mean anything underhanded or diabolical. I have seen the Jesuit described as strictly a cloak-and-dagger man, slinking about corridors musty with intrigue. A Jesuit friend of mine, too, Father Ed Moody, told me he had had this same experience. In fact, the books he had read, portraying Jesuits as schemers, plotters, and the brains behind the brains, had given him an interest in the Jesuits and he had said to himself, "That's for me." Disappointingly, he discovered, of course, that the cloak-and-dagger department exists only in books or in the minds of very young Jesuit novices prowling about the dark basements of old novitiates.

Then, too, neither do the friends of the Society always know whereof they speak. Kate O'Brien, for instance, in an essay on St. Francis Xavier in the book *Saints for Now,* remarks that the Jesuit is "under a strictly impersonal discipline." Any Jesuit knows that the discipline he is under is usually far from impersonal. In fact, there may be occasions when he wishes it were more impersonal.

Again, there are those who have portrayed the Jesuit as resembling a man from Mars, boasting a large bare green head with two blinking light bulbs in place of ears. Others have portrayed him as an efficiency expert of some sort. Still others have endowed him with super-human powers of concentration.

Now I admit that there are some Jesuits who have necessarily taken part in activities which may have made them seem members of the cloak-and-dagger division.* I also admit that a Jesuit can feel, at times, that he is under a very "impersonal discipline" indeed. I concede, too, that there really are some Jesuits who do resemble men from Mars, though their heads are more often pink or glistening white rather than green. There are some, too, who are definitely efficiency experts. And we have a few geniuses, though I am not acquainted with any

---

* It must be stated, however, that Jesuits who have been known to slink around musty corridors have done so either to save their necks or because the corridors of many Jesuit houses are simply too old not to be musty, and anything moving in them might be said to slink.

Jesuits boasting superhuman powers of concentration.*

But, with all these admissions, it must be added that these resemblances are strictly coincidental and rare. I want to write here of the Jesuit I know best, the ordinary garden variety of Jesuit. And I think I am in a good position to write about him because not too long ago I completed the Jesuit course of training and studies and am now a full-grown, if not fully matured, Jesuit.

Others have written of their professions — doctors, lawyers, men like Private Hargrove and Willie Mauldin. Then, too, Father X and Father Leo Trese have written of the diocesan priesthood. So why shouldn't I, who am a Jesuit, write about *my* profession and *my* life?

One can get a very good idea of the nature and purpose of the Society of Jesus, of its origin and history, from any number of good sources. I do not dare or care to compete with the authors of these tomes, but would prefer to speak here of the lighter side of a Jesuit's training, to portray the enjoyable, happy times we Jesuits have known in our lengthy course of studies, to point out that we do not ordinarily pursue our course with clenched teeth and jutting jaw.

I would like to tell here what I know of a Jesuit's essence, of what makes him tick, and of the things that perhaps make him sick. Unfortunately, such books on

---

* I have been informed, however, of one Jesuit who had developed his powers of concentration to a high degree. On one occasion, he was pacing up and down the deck of a banana boat in Central American waters, reading his Breviary. Since there was no rail on the craft, in an unguarded moment, he walked off the end of the boat as he read. Immediately, of course, he went under water, but witnesses are prepared

the religious life are usually written by those who are no longer living the life they describe. Such were Monica Baldwin's *I Leap Over the Wall* and Gary MacEoin's *Nothing Is Quite Enough*. Such works cannot help showing the influence of their author's divorce from the life they describe. High time we heard from someone unaware of any wall.

There are, as you know, three classes of Jesuit: Jesuit priests, brothers, and scholastics. The last-named species is a sort of baby Jesuit growing up into a priest. The young Jesuit is called a "scholastic" from his entrance into the Society until his ordination as a priest. Since I am a Jesuit priest, I shall treat here only of the life of scholastic and priest.

About the life of our brothers, suffice it to say that theirs is a humble vocation and as great as it is humble. They faithfully take care of all our material needs, day in and day out, not for any pay nor because of any special devotion to us, but for the love of God. They are truly great men, real unsung heroes.

---

to swear that when he bobbed up to the surface he imperturbably turned a page of his book. Unfortunately, I have not been able to trace the witnesses of this phenomenon to date.

Then there was that other Jesuit who wandered into the College Church (the Church of St. Francis Xavier) in St. Louis one evening during Holy Week, curious as to who was giving the sermon and anxious to hear it. Despite this inauspicious beginning, he gave a fine sermon.

I am not certain whether the two-car collision which once occurred on an open South Dakota prairie was due to over-concentration or not. At any rate, I understand that two Jesuit drivers once met in this way, with no other cars or even trees around for miles.

In this book I should like to trace the Jesuit back to his sources: Where did he first appear? Under a microscope or a rock? Did he hatch from an egg? Did he just suddenly appear one day in a cassock, or did he start out much as anyone else starts out, in a diaper? Was he fastened upon early in life by some hardened Jesuit and so trained that he could be nothing else? Or was he perhaps sold by his parents, at an early age, to the General of the Jesuits? Or did the Jesuits conspire to take away the old homestead unless this boy would promise to join their Society? Or, looking at it another way, did this young man, after an early life spent in crime, decide to enter the Society of Jesus as a refuge, as romantic tradition tells us one signs up for the French Foreign Legion? These and other similarly serious questions I should like to answer.

Then, I should like to take a glance at the Jesuit course of training and study. How does the production line turn out Jesuits? Are they indoctrinated, propagandized morning and night? Do loud-speakers blare into their ears the nefarious principles of St. Ignatius at every waking moment? And does a television camera in their room keep them constantly before the eyes of their superiors while a sign on the wall proclaims "Big Brother is watching you"? Is the course of training and study in the Society an impersonal thing? Is the final Jesuit product just a big brain moved around by legs, no different at all from the brain next to him or it?

I should like, here, to look at two sides of the Jesuit: the outside which you see (and this will necessarily consist of a light and a serious side) and the inside which you cannot see but which you can only guess at.

In these pages, too, I wish to ramble on a bit about a class which the army calls its "brass" but which the Society knows more significantly as her superiors. I would like to describe them as they are, so that the reader can judge for himself whether or not they are the automatons they have sometimes been pictured.

I might as well admit right now that this is a labor of love. Some years ago, Father Dan Lord, S.J., wrote a book entitled *My Mother*. It was a lovely book, about a lovely person, Mrs. Lord. I only wish that I could write as good a book about another lovely mother, the Society of Jesus.

As I look back on the course of training in the Society, the various stories of my companions and friends there remind me of the words of Old Font in Bryan Mac-Mahon's *Children of the Rainbow:* "The time I speak of, our lives were so thronged with small beauties that you wouldn't think 'twas sons an' daughters of the flesh we were, but children of the rainbow dwellin' always in the mornin' of the world!"

This explains, too, why I have chosen such a peculiar title for this book. Various more gruesome titles came to mind, such as *Terrible Tales of Jesuit Intrigue* or *Twenty Years of Captivity* or *I Was Hypnotized by a Jesuit*. But, while any such title would probably help to sell the book, it would also be misleading. With all the work and sweat that have been part of the past twenty years or so, there has been so much enjoyment that I could not call the account of those years anything other than *I'll Die Laughing!*

. . . or does he just suddenly appear somewhere?

A kindly Jesuit sizes up and encourages the applicant.

1

IT TAKES fifteen years to become a Jesuit priest, so you have to start fairly early if you're going to live that long. And so it was, that on a hot August day in Omaha (116 degrees), another potential Jesuit and I traded dry Omaha heat for a soggy St. Louis heat. This was in 1936.

I remember when I was leaving the Omaha Union Station, my father, charitable Irishman that he was, acted as if he was going to miss me. My leaving seemed serious also to two good friends who were at the depot when the train stopped at Council Bluffs. One of them gave me a letter containing all the things he wanted to say — the good wishes and the pledges of continued friendship and prayers. But it also seemed to portend a permanent and complete separation. The general idea everyone seemed to have was that I was doing a very brave thing, going off into voluntary exile. To me it seemed more like an adventure of sorts, one that might prove to be a dud, sure, but nevertheless an adventure. And it was more characterized by curiosity than by bravery. The separations were not easy, but the mystery of what lay ahead neutralized the pain.

My companion and I had quite a time just before
going to St. Stanislaus Seminary, Florissant, Missouri, to
begin our Novitiate. Both of us figured that we would
never have much fun again. And so we had planned on
an extra two days in St. Louis before being committed
at Florissant. We ate as though we would never eat again
(which was probably the most ironical twist of all our
spree, since I've been eating like a hog ever since). We
took in every possible event we could — movies, clubs,
the St. Louis Municipal Opera, where we saw the musical
version of *A Connecticut Yankee*. We had box seats, I
recall, at the opera, which happens to be out of doors.
About one third of the way through the performance, a
light rain began to fall. An old couple next to us, hear-
ing our muttered complaints, told us not to worry because we would be given rain checks if the performance
was halted. They didn't realize that a rain check for this
show would do us about as much good as it would the
occupant of a death cell.

The next morning we called the seminary to inform
them that two of their more promising new recruits were
groping their way toward Florissant and would appreciate
transportation the rest of the way. We were told, without any indication of the overwhelming enthusiasm we
had expected, to report to St. Louis University. At the
university we were given our lunch, complete with a
glass of beer. Things were looking up, as far as we were
concerned, as long as they served beer. We didn't know
then that it was the last beer we'd see for four years.

A young cleric, who didn't look like a young cleric
at all since he wore a blue suit, gave us a ride out to

the seminary, which is about twenty miles from St. Louis. The cleric was Father Lou Cervantes* who happens to live just down the hall from me now, almost twenty years later.

Most of us said later that had we had our own cars with us when we came to Florissant and got our first look at the place, we would have pointed our radiators in the other direction and gotten out of there as quickly as possible. The main building, the Rock Building, was one hundred years old then. They bragged about it. It looked exactly like any other hundred-year-old prison. Bravely enough, however, we went up the steps and through the front door. It groaned shut behind us.

We were no sooner inside than a tall gray-haired man, with eyes that seemed to look right through us without missing anything on the way through, greeted us. This was Father Al Hahn, our Master of Novices. At the moment he looked like the warden. But I knew him later, a very short time later, as one of the kindest, most spiritual of men. He is still one of my closest friends, and we happen to be members of the same community.

---

* In order to avoid even worse confusion, I will refer to those of my contemporaries who are now priests as "Father," even if the particular anecdote shall have taken place when they were known by some other title. In the Novitiate, we called each other "Brother," which is a very nice title, if you consider its deeper meaning and do not imagine only the relationship of lodge brothers. In an earlier day, and again today, the novices call each other "Carissime," which I imagine most American Jesuits would translate as "Pal." After his vows, the young Jesuit is known as "Mister" until he is ordained. From the time of his ordination on, he will be known as "Father," again a very significant title.

Then we were introduced to our new companions. There were seven of us altogether who were entering the Novitiate on this particular day. (Seventeen more were to come a few weeks later.) Of the seven, my companion and I were from Omaha. We were just ordinary kids, my companion directly out of high school and I with some college behind me. There were two St. Louis men, one a high school boy, the other a college graduate. There was an engineer from South Dakota and a very brilliant young man from Illinois. The other candidate was from Milwaukee. So, even in our little group of seven we had great variety.

Where do Jesuits come from? What kind of material are they made of? They come from almost anywhere, and they're made of almost any sort of material. The men I knew then and know now would have made good firemen, or cops, or teachers, or lawyers, or doctors, or just about anything. But they chose to become Jesuit priests.

Most of us, I would say, were extremely ordinary, but not all. My contemporaries, for example, included men from almost every walk of life. Perhaps the greatest majority of us had at one time or other thought of studying for a profession such as that of medicine. But there was one who had been a police sergeant.* Another had been a quarterback on the St. Mary's football team, in California. There were plenty who had been outstanding athletes. One had been named on an All-American basket-

* Occasionally, the sarge would revert to type. At least, on one occasion our superior at St. Louis was horrified to look out the window and see one of his subjects directing traffic!

ball team. Two or three had been traveling salesmen. There were a couple of orchestra leaders. One man had been a baker for a number of years. A few had been boxers. Another had made quite a name as a dancer. There was a lawyer and a male nurse. Since the war there have been all kinds of ex-G.I.'s.

Many of the men were from Jesuit schools, but four of my companions had never seen a Jesuit before. We had many from Catholic colleges, many from state universities. And, sometime before my entrance into the Society, we had had Father Henry Sutti, a product of Father Flanagan's Boys Town. They came from all over, and exactly why they had come, half of them couldn't have told you in so many words.

We varied in physical characteristics as much as we did in origin. Some were small, some large, some young, some older. For the most part we were all Americans, but we varied widely in ancestry. Of the seven of us, for example, who entered on that August 8, 1936, there was one Bohemian, one Pole, three Germans, and two Irishmen. And as we varied in "nationality," we also varied in temperament. I think that we proved, just that small group of us, that there are many more than the classic four temperaments.

But with all of us coming from such different walks of life and being blessed or cursed with so many different temperaments, there must have been some common element that brought us all together, some common purpose for which we came. Naturally, there was such a purpose, such a common element — a vocation to the Society of Jesus.

I do not know enough about the theology of a vocation to write with any authority about it. But it is important, nevertheless, to have some basic notion of what this mysterious thing called a vocation really is and what it is not.

The first thing to remember is that one's state of life *is* his vocation, or his "calling" in life. And so, if you're a businessman or a housewife, that is your vocation. And if a person is called to be a priest or a religious, that is his vocation. Your vocation is nothing more than the special function in life God has best fitted you for and into which He has directed you, but not forced you, by His providence. It is the state of life in which you can best serve Him and most efficiently save your soul.

In this book, however, I'm going to use the word in a most restricted sense. So when I say "vocation" in these pages I'll mean the call to be a Jesuit priest.

Many people, among them many who should know better, automatically consider as vocation fodder the young man who is very devout outwardly. If he makes an extra visit to the church, if he prays with a beatific smile upon his angelic countenance or with a certain pious twist to his head, if he is interested in the "things of the spirit" — then he has a vocation. The boy who has no interest or no particular interest in sports and is, above all, interested in study to the extent that this is his chief pleasure, this paragon is supposed, by self-constituted authorities, to have a vocation.* The lad

---

* Fortunately, today there are few people who think that physical weakness and a vocation go hand in hand. There is a farmer just outside St. Louis who will never have that

who is somewhat of a hermit and who is horrified at the very thought of speaking to a girl is obviously destined for the priesthood. Or perhaps the boy who has a vocation is simply one who couldn't get another job.

Yes, the people who are sure they know most about it — those who have never so much as bothered to speak to a priest except in a crowd — these authorities *know* that there has to be something a little queer about the young man with a vocation. Above all, they'll tell you, he must be a whiz at external piety, kind to old ladies — taking care that they are plenty old — and so forth.

These people seem to believe also that one's actual calling to the religious life has to be accomplished by a direct personal invitation from the Holy Spirit. Perhaps an angel could do the job if the Holy Spirit were busy elsewhere at the moment, but there must be this mysterious spiritual call. Joan of Arc had nothing on the potential religious.

Such theories are, of course, laughable to anyone who has even the slightest knowledge of a vocation. I have never yet encountered anyone who persevered in his vocation who was overpious before entering on it. In

---

idea again, if he ever did have. Another scholastic and I were cutting down trees with the man one day. My fellow scholastic had never felled a tree in his life, but he thought it was fun anyhow. The tree we were working on started to go when the farmer yelled, "Hey, look out! It's going the wrong way." My companion calmly walked around the tree and pushed it so that it fell in the right direction. The vocal admiration of our friend the farmer was a little too emphatic to repeat here. But he was the only one surprised. I had seen my friend do much more remarkable things than pushing a tree around.

fact, only a relative few have been endowed with slightly more than ordinary genuine piety at the beginning of their religious life.

Nor was it ever a question of not being able to get any other job. The men I have known in the Society of Jesus could, for the most part, have succeeded in any walk of life.

Finally, had any of us waited for a personal invitation from the Holy Spirit, he would still be standing outside with his ears cocked.

A vocation, on the contrary, is a very simple thing. True, it is some sort of "calling." A religious vocation really is a call from God, a call to serve Him more exclusively. But God does not usually issue His orders directly. Instead of giving each one an individual, vocal invitation, He calls him in the same way He does just about everything else — by His providence or by ordering the natural events of life so as to accomplish His purpose.

There are certain signs or indications by which a man knows whether he could be a doctor or a lawyer or a professional athlete or an insurance salesman or a singer or a garbage collector. And there will also be certain signs which will tell him he is not cut out for a particular profession. He should, for example, give up any idea of being a professional singer if he can't hold a note in a bathtub.

When a person applies for any job at all, the first thing that must be learned is whether he has the ability to perform the duties of that position. A religious vocation is no exception, naturally, to this common-sense rule. And the signs which indicate a religious vocation or the lack of it are very, very ordinary things. If a young man has enough intelligence to cope with the course of studies in the Society of Jesus, that is one sign that he has a vocation to be a Jesuit. This is not to say, by any means, that he must be a genius. We would be in a sad way indeed with thirty thousand geniuses! He must have, perhaps, a little more than ordinary intelligence and a little more than the ordinary ability to work, to plug away even when the going is difficult. The Society does not accept anyone who has not finished four years of high school, chiefly because it would be difficult before that time for a young man to be certain of what he wanted and for the Society to be certain she wanted him.

As a part of the necessary ability, of course, the young man must be living an upright life. Not an overpious life, certainly, but a life in which he is striving to remain free from serious sin.

Besides the intellectual and moral ability, the young man must also have the necessary health to go through a life of study. Some religious orders have a longer course to accomplish than others. In the Society of Jesus, one must go through a fifteen-year course of study, so his health should be sturdy.

As a further sign of a vocation, as an indication of God's will, the candidate must have a proper intention. This means, first of all, that he must have the desire to serve God in a particular vocation. This desire, really, is very often nothing more than the willingness to give it a serious try. It is rarely an overwhelming thing. And it is even more rarely unaccompanied by *some* misgivings. But at least a rudimentary desire to serve God must be there, because the Jesuit army is made up entirely of volunteers. No one is drafted.

Besides the desire, there must also be a proper motive for wishing to enter the religious life. You do not, for instance, find young men becoming Jesuits because of broken hearts. Nor do you find them entering the religious life as an escape of any sort. But if, by some miracle, they were accepted, they could not last two weeks on such a motive.

The motive need not, of course, be any especially lofty ideal. It might simply be that the young man is convinced that the best way for him to save his soul is in the religious life. Or he might possibly have a higher motive, wishing genuinely to serve God more perfectly and to bring others to do the same. But any worth-while supernatural motive is enough. So, if a young man has enough ability, sufficient health, and the right intention, he can be a Jesuit, even without showing a passport from the Holy Spirit. Or rather, his ability, health, and intention are passport enough. Four Jesuit examiners talk with him in separate interviews to make sure he has a vocation. Their individual opinions, together with the candidate's academic record and the results of his physical exams, are sent to the Jesuit Provincial. If the Provincial feels that the applicant can make the grade, he tells him to come and try it. He tries it and is tried for two years in the Jesuit Novitiate.

II

ABOUT the best you could say for the Rock Building was that it looked like a jail. It still does.

We didn't realize that day, as we walked through the door of the Rock Building, that there were other buildings on the property which we would have much more to do with. It loomed at us too much for us to notice anything else. And, incidentally, it still looms today. The shutters have been painted a nice shade of blue, thus relieving the institutional atmosphere somewhat. It now resembles a prison with blue shutters.*

But I guess that the old Rock Building's resemblance to a prison is just one of those things that the good Lord wants prospective novices to face and conquer. It took only a very short time to find that the atmosphere of the place had nothing in common with its appearance.

---

* In all fairness to the good old Rock Building, I should add that there are those, among them a very fine architect, who consider it a thing of beauty and a joy forever, with none of the prison aspect I mention. Aesthetically, I bow before their better judgment, but my first impression stubbornly persists.

The Novitiate seems a warm, homey place.

We freely entered the door and we could have walked out (in fact, some did) with equal freedom at any time.

For the first two years of his religious training, the candidate for the Society of Jesus undergoes what is called the Novitiate. Here he is taught to pray. Here he learns just what is the spirit of this Society of Jesus at whose door he's knocking. If, at the end of two years, he decides that he really wants to be a Jesuit, and if the Society agrees that he should be, he is allowed to pronounce his perpetual vows, by which he promises God that he will live the rest of his life observing poverty, chastity, and obedience as a Jesuit. If, however, at any time during those two years he decides that this life is not for him or if the Society decides that he cannot fit into her scheme of things or capture her spirit, he freely leaves.

Contrary to some "historical" sources, the prospective Jesuit does not learn, during his Novitiate, means of political intrigue and how to wear a cloak and sport a dagger.* The purpose of the Novitiate is rather to learn what it means to be a Jesuit and to begin to practice the principles upon which the Jesuit life is built.

Briefly, what *does* it mean to be a Jesuit, a member of the Society of Jesus?

In itself, the Society of Jesus is an army of men whose

---

* In all fairness, I should say that there are Jesuits who wear cloaks occasionally. And they do look a bit sinister, too. To date, however, I have not seen one with a dagger, though I have observed one recently with a rather vicious-looking pocketknife which he makes use of when the meat is too tough for the ordinary knife.

purpose is outlined with perfect clarity in their rules, "the salvation and perfection of their own soul and the salvation and perfection of their neighbor with the divine grace." And again, "Let us all be of one mind. . . ." In other words, there is a single purpose, common to all members of the Society. This purpose is most succinctly stated in the Latin motto, *Ad Majorem Dei Gloriam* (usually abbreviated *A.M.D.G.*), which simply means "All for the greater glory of God."

But if we consider the Society of Jesus an army, we must also keep in mind how it differs from an army. The Society has a spirit far different from that of a fighting army with a material purpose. We Jesuits are under a King who loves each one of us, Christ. This King has given us the express command to love one another, a command echoed by St. Ignatius when he wrote in the very first rule of the Society that "The interior law of charity and love is to help thereunto [that is, to the attaining of our purpose] rather than any exterior constitutions."

To be a Jesuit means to live in the close companionship of Christ. It means to be a member of an army of which Christ is the King and St. Ignatius the General. But it means more than to be a G.I. in a spiritual army, because there is an element involved that is not found in an army. In this army, one lives a life of *joyful* service, a life of love with the co-operation of those around him and above him. I have often watched people on a bus or walking along the street and have been impressed by their grimness. You do not find that among a busload of Jesuits. Rather, the thing you notice most is their joy in a common worth-while purpose and in the companionship of those who share that purpose.

Like the soldier, the Jesuit has to take orders. He has to go wherever and whenever he is sent. This means that he must necessarily be detached as completely as possible from any particular place, persons, or type of work. He could be a Ph.D. in Greek and be told to teach mathematics, though, it should be added, this would rarely happen. He might be a great preacher and be given the job of writing. It all depends on where he is most needed at the time for God's greater glory. No other system could logically fit the purpose of the Society.

The Jesuit has all kinds of means at his disposal for attaining his purpose: the salvation of his own soul and that of his neighbor. He does quite a number of spiritual push-ups every day, including an hour of mental prayer each morning. He is encouraged and helped to attain as close as possible a union with God in prayer. He is also encouraged to attain as complete a union as possible with the suffering Christ, through sacrifice, mortification, and penance. He is to become so completely detached from the things around him that he will be "as one who being dead to the world and to self-love lives only to Christ our Lord."

The young Jesuit is taught that he must imitate in his life, not the world he has left, but Christ whom he has come to serve. The rule tells him that he must learn to "abhor wholly and not in part what the world loves and embraces and to accept and desire with his whole strength whatsoever Christ our Lord loved and embraced. For as worldly men who follow the things of the world love and with great diligence seek honors, reputation, and the credit of a great name upon earth as the world teaches them, so those who follow Christ must seek slanders and injuries and wish to be held and accounted as fools without at the same time giving any occasion for it, in imitation of Christ." The Jesuit is taught that it is not always the better thing to defend oneself, even if accused falsely, though there may be occasions when the truth should or must appear. Certainly it is more perfect, at times at least, to suffer even false accusations in silence, in imitation of Christ.

The Jesuit is supposed to seek always his "greater abnegation and continual mortification." He is not merely to resist any temptation to sin that comes his way, but he is to fight against it by cultivating the opposite virtue. He is to bring the war into the enemy's camp. Thus, if a man tends to be proud, he is not merely to fight against pride but he is to develop humility.

He is to cultivate a perfect set of values so that first things are always put first. He is, therefore, to consider spiritual gifts and virtues "of greater moment than either learning or other natural or human gifts."

He is to be poor with Christ, so that his "diet, apparel, and lodging will be such as become poor men," and he is to seek for his own use "the meanest things of the house." In this way, he will more easily imitate the humility of Christ and consider everyone about him as his superior.

In his imitation of Christ, the Jesuit is to be especially perfect in his obedience, so much so that he considers the orders he is given, not as coming from any human being, but from God Himself. He reasons that God's providence has put him where he is and that the same providence has put the superior where *he* is. Naturally, then, God must intend the superior's commands to be obeyed.

His humility is to carry over from his own personal life to his attitude toward the Society. While he knows that for him the Society is the only life, still he will look upon it, with respect to other orders, as the least of all.

Finally, Jesuits can and should be described in a paragraph which is known as the *Sum and Scope of the Constitutions:*

Men crucified to the world, and to whom the world itself is crucified, such would the rule of our life have us to be; new men, I say, who have put off their affections to put on Christ; dead to themselves, to live to justice; who, with St. Paul, in labors, in watchings, in fastings, in chastity, in knowledge, in long-suffering, in sweetness, in the Holy Ghost, in charity unfeigned, in the word of truth, show themselves ministers of God; and by the armor of justice on the right hand, and on the left, by honor and dishonor, by evil report and good report, by good success finally and ill success, press forward with great strides to their heavenly country, and by all means possible and with all zeal, urge on others also, ever looking to God's greater glory. This is the sum and aim of our Institute.

This is what a Jesuit novice is told to aim at for the rest of his life.

Some time ago, in one of its "Letters to the Editor," *Time,* the weekly news magazine, printed a letter from someone who decried the Catholic clergy because they "wallowed in luxury." I could not help thinking, on reading this authoritative communication, of the "luxury" we had wallowed in as novices.

The building in which we spent the two luxurious years of our Novitiate had been built in 1873, and no one had seen fit to improve upon it since, except to put steel rods through it to hold it together.

There were two dormitories for the novices, quite plush affairs done in old Missouri decorations. I do not recall that the walls were even painted, but I'm sure they had been at one time, perhaps by the pioneer missionary, Father DeSmet, just before he died in 1873. Each of us had a bed and a washstand which also served as a wardrobe. A series of pipes about seven feet high ran between and along the front of the beds. Curtains were hung by rings from these pipes so that, when it wasn't too warm, we could have a certain amount of privacy. These were the gorgeous surroundings of our sleeping quarters. Today, with the old building gone, I suppose that those who think that we wallow in luxury would be quite shocked to find that the novices now sleep in individual cubicles. These tub-thumpers for poverty would be cheered to know, however, that the novices still have to go outside their cubicles to get wash water, as there is no running water. I do not know if the novices have our winter difficulties today with that wash water. Frequently we had to get up in the morning and pitch the whole thing out. It's pretty hard to work up a lather in ice.

We also studied and read together, without any privacy

The food is served with a delicate sense of taste and finesse.

whatsoever, in one big room called the "ascetory." This, too, was a luxurious room. When the Missouri trade winds were blowing, you could close all the windows and shutters, and it was still impossible to keep papers on your desk because of the breeze whipping through the room. Occasionally (it seemed much more often than that) I got the job of sweeping this room or the dormitories. To keep the dust down, we first sprinkled the floors with scobs (wet sawdust). Most of us soon discovered that if we swept with the grain we had a great number of scobs to throw out. But if we swept against the grain we never needed a dustpan, because scobs and dirt alike only served to fill up the cracks in the floor.

We sported, too, a rather snappy wardrobe. The pants we were given could appropriately have had a number stamped on them. We were also given what were called *manualia* (work) jackets. These were very attractive prison-gray blazers boasting all the clever tailoring of a sack. They did not come in too many sizes, so that as a result they really did something for the shorter and longer ones among us.

The food stacked before us was worth the trip to Missouri. Certainly it would have shocked any given customer of the Waldorf. But it was good, substantial food and there was always plenty of it. Three times a week, we had corn bread and stew for breakfast. The number of square feet of corn bread and number of barrels of stew consumed over the course of a year would probably astonish even Ripley.

Today the old buildings have gone and, I believe, our old prisonlike wardrobe. This is good, of course. But we wouldn't have wanted it any other way than the way we had it. It was not only enjoyable but, at the same time, gave us some practical occasion for turning the theory of the vow of poverty into practice. And, besides, it gave us that little touch of Spartan training which is good for anyone.

The grounds of St. Stanislaus Seminary are and always have been extensive and attractive. There is a huge garden, with all kinds of beautiful trees, a vineyard extending down toward the highway, and a large field where we played such things as baseball, basketball, handball, tennis, and touch football.

Besides the Rock Building, there were the Novitiate, the Juniorate, the infirmary, the chapel and refectory, the winery, the laundry, the dairy, the powerhouse, and various other smaller buildings. Between the larger buildings was an open quadrangle, or courtyard, containing several cisterns holding drinking water. The cisterns weren't a bad idea, since the piped water in the buildings was unfit for human consumption. Then, too, if we cared to and preferred soft water for washing, we could fill our washbasins at the pump and do a balancing act to the dormitory on the third floor.

Back of the seminary — that is, to the west — the property extends for two miles, more or less, through St. Joseph's Woods and out to Charbonierre, our villa on the Missouri River. Here the juniors went each Thursday. But the novices enjoyed this privilege only a few times a year.

We ran into a lot of new things as novices; in fact, everything was new to us. Some things which we had considered perfectly normal before were not allowed us

now. For example, we were told that we had exactly
one week to break the smoking habit. And this we did,
somehow, with the greatest of ease. One of my contemporaries probably took longer than most people, since
he always seemed to have a few packs of cigarettes left
after each shakedown. Finally, however, even this supply
ran out.

The first week at Florissant is known as the week of
First Probation. It was during this time that we tried to
get somewhat used to the place, before receiving our
cassocks at the end of the week. But, of course, you
can't get used to something like that in a week. During
this time, one of the second-year novices shepherded us
around and tried to acquaint us with the nooks and
crannies. This chosen one's job is not always easy.
Father Walter Harris, I am told, had a very fine time
during this week when he first came to Florissant. But
his angel (the second-year novice who has charge of
the First Probationers) did not find things so easy. On
one occasion he approached Father Harris to tell him
that there was an instruction in five minutes, only to be
greeted with: "What do you want me to do — give it?"
Justice was satisfied, however, when Father Harris himself took on the onerous duties of an angel a year later.

A couple of years later, when his angel was trying to
explain to another potential mystic that he was supposed
to meditate for an hour on a page or so in a meditation
book, he was asked the simple question, "An hour! How
come? I can read through that in two minutes."

Anyhow, with all our stupidity and simplicity, at the
end of the week of probation, we were allowed to wear

Getting used to the cassock is no problem at all.

our cassocks.* And you never saw a prouder group in
your life. The cassock was to be our uniform from then
on, and we were glad to get inside it. We wore it at all
times except when "fatigues" were necessary or more
convenient.

With the donning of our cassocks, we began our
Novitiate. It was a life of study (but not too much of
it), of prayer (plenty of it), and of discovery. Formally,
we studied very little, because the purpose of the Novitiate is to learn the spiritual life and this is done largely
by reading, instruction, and prayer. Any studying we did
was chiefly to keep us in practice. However, we did try
our best to learn all the Latin we could during this
time, since our studies later on in philosophy and theology
would require a clear knowledge of that language. It
was for this reason that we spoke Latin to one another
for fifteen minutes of the recreation period each evening.

The daily order was such that we never found ourselves with any time on our hands. In fact, you could
never do anything at all for more than fifteen minutes
without a bell sounding and starting you off in some
other direction.

---

* The cassock is the long black robe worn by a priest. All
cassocks are long and black, but not all are the same. The
Jesuit cassock has no buttons and is held together at the
waist (the exact location of which may shift somewhat as
life goes on) by a cincture, or black sash, about two inches
wide. The cincture is wrapped around the waist twice and
is knotted at the starboard side. Both ends fall gracefully to
within a foot or two of the ground. Novices and juniors wear
a celluloid collar with this cassock. The novice also wears a
large rosary in his cincture. The trick at first is learning not
to walk up the inside of one's cassock as he goes up stairs.

We were taught during this time that work is a good thing, the more humble the job the better. We cut one another's hair, with the expected results. We scrubbed floors. We swept. We washed thousands upon thousands of dishes. And in general we worked.

We were taught to practice restraint. We were not allowed to talk except at the times assigned for recreation. And, if it was necessary to say anything during times of silence, it was to be in Latin, a regulation which discourages speaking without necessity. We were taught, too, not to be looking about at things which we really didn't have to look at — in other words, to restrain our eyes. It was very surprising to discover that we didn't miss very much even when we practiced such modesty quite well.

Naturally, there were some who made themselves menaces for a time by overdoing this "modesty of the eyes." However, they gradually got over it, after crashing into a few immovable objects and being told about it by not a few movable ones.

We had to learn, too, a whole new set of words, terms which, at first, sounded very peculiar to our ears. There was the word *manualia,* which was only a longer word for work. In my second year of Novitiate, when I was one of the athletic managers, I enjoyed much more pleasant *manualia* periods, since I was on my own. I recall during one long *manualia* session, I was lying under a tree trying to flip green apples into the tennis court marker, when the *Socius* (assistant) to the Master of Novices pulled me out of my reverie rather abruptly.

Then there was the word *flexoria* which was a more

complicated way of saying a half hour of meditation. There were the words *jentaculum*, *prandium*, and *coena*, quite innocent in themselves since they meant breakfast, dinner, and supper. They took on a sinister meaning, however, when the word *post* was put before them, because then they simply meant that we *worked* after breakfast, dinner, or supper. Then there was the delightful word *haustus*, which indicates a fine old custom in the Society of grabbing a little snack in the middle of the afternoon to tide one over until supper. I have found that particular custom very easy to observe throughout the years.

We had what were called *toni* classes once a week. A *toni* class is a speech class, and I think all of us found it extremely difficult to speak before our own men. But it certainly made public speaking easier later on. Once you've spoken to a bunch of people who sit there taking notes on what you're doing wrong, it isn't too hard to speak before a less obviously critical group.

Much more of our time was taken up by prayer than we had ever thought possible. As a result, when we finally did get a chance to go swimming at Charbonierre, the relative length and breadth and depth of the calluses on our knees became a subject of lengthy speculation.

We did not, of course, take to such a life like ducks to water. Some did seem to fit in perfectly from the very beginning. But for most of us, it was like getting into a tub of very cold water, and we preferred to slide in gradually. A couple of us, for example, saw nothing at all wrong at first in standing on the highway and whistling at the girls who went by in cars, much to the disedification of the second-year novice who accompanied us. Some saw no reason to mark their clothes with the number they were assigned, because they figured they wouldn't want their clothes inked up that way when they left in about a week. And these, strangely enough, were the very ones who did persevere.

I recall the first time I answered one of our second-year novices in English when I should have been speaking Latin. You can imagine his shocked surprise when to his demand, *"Latine, Frater,"* I asked him simply, "What the hell for?" I soon learned what for! It took some time, too, to get used to calling one another *"Frater,"* the Latin word for "Brother."

No, we were by no means finished Jesuits to start with. Most of us really had no idea of what the religious life was like. The only thing that saved us was the fact that we were willing to learn, and we had a Novice Master who was quite willing and completely capable of teaching us.

Difficult as it was for us to adjust ourselves, it all came down to one question: "Do you want it enough to be willing to learn?" We did and we were. At the beginning of the month of October of our first year of Novitiate, we underwent something that marked the beginning of our change to a spiritual outlook on things: the long retreat of thirty days, during which we conversed only with God and not with one another. It marked the beginning of God's taking everything we had and helping us to turn it in His direction.

Jesuits, we found during the long retreat, are a sort of light-horse cavalry or marine corps of God. They must be ready to go anywhere where there is hope of doing good for God and His Church. They must wish to signalize themselves in His service. We, it is true, were only recruits in this army of Christ. We were raw material, yes — plenty raw. But we had the energy and the ambition, and we were willing to do our part if we could be shown how. The long retreat was the first big help we had in getting our noses pointed in the right direction.

The long retreat is based on the *Spiritual Exercises* of St. Ignatius Loyola, who also happens to have been the founder of the Society of Jesus. The month of the long retreat is spent meditating on the truths outlined in these *Exercises*.

St. Ignatius, once a soldier himself, certainly let his own spirit shine through his book. As we studied the *Exercises*, we began to look upon Christ's work as the work of a spiritual army, seeing Christ as our King and Leader, and Satan (and very often ourselves) as His enemy and ours. We studied and prayed to understand the personality of Christ, our King, until we came, gradually, to love Him and to be willing to fight anything opposed to Him. We saw more definitely that we would have to make certain sacrifices for Him if we were to get anywhere in His service. And we saw, above all, that the best way to serve Him was to imitate Him.

After our long retreat, we spent the rest of our two years of Novitiate trying to put the principles we had learned there into practice. We tried, too, to make absolutely sure, as we approached the day of our vows, whether this was what we really wanted for the rest of our lives. The great majority of us decided that it was.

But the Novitiate was by no means all work. We took long and frequent walks over a Missouri countryside, which is especially lovely in the autumn. We took part in every sport ever invented and a few of our own. We did everything to keep a healthy mind and a healthy body. And we enjoyed each other's company tremendously. It was a good life, a happy life, one filled with peace and camaraderie.

October of our second year of Novitiate was especially pleasant. During this time we were with those of our own group only, unhampered and unbothered by the first-year men, who were busy with their long retreat. Our pleasures were simple but memorable — made up of hearty and hilarious recreations. We were very happy young men and gave scarcely a thought to the more sophisticated worldly pleasures we had left behind.

At the end of our two years of trial, after the long retreat, two eight-day retreats, five three-day retreats, and innumerable days of recollection, countless hours of meditation and spiritual reading, and numerous conferences with our Master of Novices, we were allowed to take our three vows of poverty, chastity, and obedience, by which we promised to observe those vows as Jesuits forever. And our vow day certainly was one of the happiest days of our lives.

It would not be fair to end this chapter on the Novitiate without a very brief tribute to the man who trained us for that day, Father Al Hahn, our Master of Novices. He made us love the Society. He taught us to love God above all things and to live for God. And what more could one ask of any man?

III

AT THE end of his two years of Novitiate, the adolescent Jesuit pronounces his perpetual vows of poverty, chastity, and obedience in the Society of Jesus. He then passes from the Novitiate to the Juniorate. And as he trots happily across the bridge,* we'd better take a short look at these vows of poverty, chastity, and obedience.

A vow, first of all, is a promise freely made to God, a promise to do something good, something which is *better*, in fact, than its opposite. So I can make a vow to give to the poor every Christmas, but I can't make a vow to murder my congressman. On second thought, let's use a

---

* Since there are usually many buildings in a Jesuit establishment, and since there is ordinarily a good deal of traffic between these buildings, enclosed bridges usually join them, so that a man can run the bridge to his heart's content in all types of weather. Thus, at Florissant in our day, one such bridge connected the Novitiate and the Rock Building, another the Rock Building and the infirmary, another the Rock Building and the Juniorate, another the Juniorate and the chapel, another the Novitiate and the infirmary, and another the Novitiate and the chapel. I am not sure just what a psychiatrist would have to say about all this.

completely unlikely example and say I can't take a vow to murder my mother.

Since a promise is always a solemn thing and since a promise made to God is so much more dignified than one made to a man, a vow carries with it a very solemn obligation.

A vow may be either temporary or perpetual, depending on how long the vower wishes it to bind.

After two years of Novitiate, the young Jesuit makes three such vows or solemn promises to God. In his case, they are not temporary but perpetual. He intends to bind himself by them for life.

And the first vow he takes is that of *poverty*. By this vow, he gives up the possession, or at least the use, of any property. In the Society, this means that if he wants even so much as a bus token, he must ask the Superior for it. (This does not mean, of course, that the Superior may not give him a dozen bus tokens at once.) The vow of poverty is a vow of dependence rather than a vow to embrace actual abject poverty. But this vow of dependence supposes that the abject poverty will be accepted willingly, should it come, as it sometimes does.

By the vow of *chastity*, the religious binds himself, under an extra obligation, to observe those commandments of God which forbid any unlawful use of sex. And the vow of chastity goes one tremendous step further. By it, the religious promises God to forego even the lawful right to marriage.*

---

* Since the religious foregoes by such a solemn promise the right to marriage, it would be very foolish for him to run the risk of falling in love. It is for this reason that safe-

I am sure there are lots of people who think the vows of poverty and obedience are wonderful things, but who look upon the vow of chastity as foolishness. But there are many reasons for a religious to take this vow. Without enumerating minor reasons, let's mention only the most important ones. First of all, there is no greater help for him to give his *undivided* attention to God and to his work. And, second, the religious life is a life of the love of God. What better way to *show* his love for God than by voluntarily relinquishing not only the most monopolistic human love but also the greatest human pleasure? We show how much we love by how much we are willing to sacrifice.

I have had quite enough of would-be authorities who either consider the vow of chastity as a sign of misogynism or knowingly and leeringly proclaim it can't be done. In the first place, there are no more religious misogynists than lay misogynists, probably not nearly so many.* Chastity is the vow by which we keep our

---

guards must be taken which might seem slight and over-cautious to others, but which are quite necessary. We are human beings. Only a fool fails to realize that he can best avoid the things he likes, if avoid them he should, by keeping them at a distance. This has nothing in common with prudishness, scrupulosity, or misogynism.

* It may also come as a surprise to some people that most Jesuits are quite fond of small children. I am, too, except that I am also afraid of them. One of our St. Louis University lay professors had a small daughter named Vern Alice. She was about six or seven when we were philosophers. At one of our social functions in the gym at St. Louis, two of the monks were enjoying themselves and entertaining Vern Alice at the same time. At one stage of these general festivities they were on their hands and knees before a door trying to coax

love from becoming specialized, so that we can bestow it on all men *and* women under God. And, in the second place, these paragons of virtue should not consider something impossible for others simply because it would be impossible for themselves. After all, there are people who can walk a tightrope, and those who cannot. It's largely a matter of patience, rightly placed confidence, restraint, practice, and balance.

And then there are the righteous who claim that religious with their vow of chastity are slowing up the growth of the human race. Yet these exemplars and stanch advocates of social virtue think it's perfectly fine to get married and have but one or no children.

But let's get back to our vows. The third vow the religious pronounces is that of *obedience*. And its scope is clear, I believe, from the very term. By this vow, the religious promises to live at the command of his legitimate superiors, to go where he is sent, and to do what he is told when he gets there.

It should be noted that all three vows free the religious from worldly entanglements so that he can concentrate his full attention on God and his neighbor.

These are the vows, then, that the Jesuit pronounces as he leaves the Novitiate to enter the Juniorate. Passing from Novitiate to Juniorate is variously described as "going across the bridge," "winning your biretta,"* and other

---

her to come out when a deep voice behind them brought them to their feet quite abruptly. Seems that Father Rector was curious as to what they were doing in that rather odd position at a public gathering.

* A biretta is the rather peculiar-looking three-cornered black hat you occasionally see a priest under.

The Jesuit manifests no vanity when he first tries on his biretta.

equally subtle expressions. No longer will the junior wear a rosary in his cincture as do the novices. And there will be times when he will actually be allowed to make use of his watch. So, externally, the only difference between the novice and the junior is that the novice wears a rosary in his cincture while a junior sometimes wears his head in a biretta. That is the only external difference. As far as his life is concerned, there is a great change, because the junior is beginning his long course of Jesuit studies.

In the Novitiate, at least in our day, there was — fortunately, I thought — very little formal study. We had some Latin and Greek classes which were just enough to keep us in touch with study and to give us a better foundation in those languages, but which were never allowed to become obnoxious or to interfere with our study of spiritual things, with our life of prayer.

The junior, on the other hand, plunges into a life of study. For two years the Jesuit studies the classics in the Juniorate. Then he becomes immersed in the three-year study of philosophy. After the latter three-year period, he gets a chance to apply some of the things he has learned and to test himself as a teacher, as he is sent to teach for three years in some Jesuit high school. After his teaching period or regency, he studies theology for four years, during the course of which he is ordained a priest. Finally, if he is still alive and kicking, he is subjected to what is called the Tertianship, which is similar to a final year of Novitiate. Again, during this year, he studies chiefly the spiritual life, but he also studies the Constitutions and the Institute of his Order.

It is as a junior, then, that the young Jesuit begins what appears to be a rather long grind of studies, but which is in reality so well split up and organized that the time seems very short. As a junior, he studies the "classics." That is, he saturates himself with Latin, Greek, English, history, and — as a sort of side line — modern languages. In our years as juniors, Father Ray O'Donnell and Father Francis Preuss (who was also the Dean of the Juniorate) very capably taught us Latin. Father Leonard Fencl taught us Greek. Some were actually thrilled by the poetry of Homer, the philosophy of Plato, and the oratory of Demosthenes. But I was very gently told by Father Fencl that the only way I was improving in Greek was in the speed with which I finished the exercises. And, at the time, this seemed the only desirable goal in that gorgeous language.

We were also blessed with two first-rate English teachers, Father Paul Smith, who is now head of the English Department at Creighton University, and Father Norman Dreyfus, who is now head of the English Department at St. Louis University.

The speech classes we had had in the Novitiate continued on in the Juniorate, meeting regularly once each week. In our second year of Juniorate, Father Marion Budzinski held us in suspense from one speech class to the next.

Father Al Jacobsmeyer taught us history. Father "Jake" read very widely and had the peculiar type of mind that is able to organize such reading into united, vivid, and interesting lectures. I, for one, was never any great shakes at learning history, probably because there was too much work involved. But I learned to enjoy the stuff as served up by Father Jacobsmeyer.

During the summers, we studied modern languages — German and French. I know that many of my companions learned these languages almost perfectly. Even I learned enough to pass the entrance exams for my degree work.

Mathematics, the only thing that I really wanted to study at that time, was not allowed in the Juniorate. So, probably as a sort of stopgap, I developed some slight curiosity for English literature at this time, an interest that on occasion, in the years to come, took on the vehemence and absorption of a passion. For the first time in my life, in the Juniorate, I began to read. It took a long time to make up for the things that I should have read years before, but I finally managed to eat my way through a good part of the heap of English literature.

Physically, the surroundings of the Juniorate were a slight but definite improvement on those of the Novitiate. We still slept in the same sort of large dormitories. We still studied all together in one huge room. But our building was less ancient and, therefore, seemed much neater and cleaner — and warmer.

Our lives were really much different from what they had been in the Novitiate. We were allowed a little bit more freedom, for one thing. In the Novitiate, for instance, we had been allowed only a two-hour walk twice a week. And we had been allowed to go to the field for games only once or twice a week. Now, as juniors, we were allowed either to walk or take part in the games at field an hour every day. On Thursdays, we could select a com-

The purpose of athletics is to keep a healthy mind
in a healthy body.

panion and take as long a walk as we wished. I believe that Father Gene Korth and I still hold the record for long walks, having hiked forty miles in one day.*

One of the pleasantest features of the Juniorate was the privilege of choosing one's own companion. In the Novitiate we had always walked in assigned groups of three. Now, in the Juniorate, we could go with whomever we pleased and we could go in pairs. It really didn't make much difference as far as seeing and knowing everyone was concerned, but anyone will tell you that there simply are certain days which better fit certain characters. And there are days when some characters must be avoided. It's just that some people are made to order for rainy days, some for sunshine. Besides, three *can* be a crowd.

Since the life of a junior is one of rather intensive study, everything he does tends to be equally intense. It is for this reason that anyone watching the juniors exercising at field would think he had stumbled on a sect of exercise worshipers. Some of the touch football, basketball, soccer, and baseball games looked, from a distance, like a Central American revolution. It is really surprising that so little blood was spilled.

I was once speaking to a young man in a bus depot in Leavenworth, Kansas, who told me that he had gone to school near a seminary and that he and his classmates

---

* I can see now the expressions on some Jesuit faces as they read this, Jesuits who have, perhaps, been under the illusion for years that they themselves held such a record. It is wonderful to have this opportunity to put the truth down in black and white. Those who wish to dispute this fact can write a book of their own.

played football and basketball with the seminarians occasionally. What he wanted to know was what kind of raw meat they fed seminarians, or if they fed them at all! He said they were like a bunch of hungry bears who had been just let loose and that they played as though they were going to be tossed a hunk of raw meat for every point scored. He himself, he told me, was about a fifth-string quarterback, but he got in early in the game, as his predecessors were carried out one by one.

I remember a basketball game that we had one day in St. Louis. It was a pretty good game and the score was very close. At one time, one of the monks who took his sports very seriously was driving in for a setup under the basket. One of the coeds from St. Louis University chose that particular inauspicious moment to cut across the basketball court on her way home. The driving Jesuit, all 195 pounds of him, bounced her onto the court. Being a very polite Jesuit, he helped her to her feet, bawling her out for being on the court as he did so. But, of course, he had gone in to make the basket before coming back to help her up.*

About two miles from the Jesuit Novitiate at Florissant is Charbonierre, the junior villa overlooking the Missouri River. Here, the juniors spend each Thursday of the year and two weeks of the summer. Here, they themselves do all the cooking and whatever work has to be done in

---

* The worst contests among Jesuits seem to take place on St. Patrick's day. For some reason or other, probably because the Micks all seem to be on the same side on this day, the competition gets pretty rough. At any rate, we usually had an instruction the next day on overemphasis of athletics.

keeping the place up. Here they can swim or hike or do whatever they wish.

Loving study as I always have, I found the Thursdays in the Juniorate the most pleasant days of those two years. Two or three of us would go out in a group each Thursday, either to St. Joe's Woods (through which we passed on our way to Charbonierre) or to Charbonierre itself or down by the Missouri River. We would spend the day cutting down trees, building bridges and roads, splitting up rocks, digging ditches, or whatever else needed to be done. The change helped us to face another six days of study.

As juniors, we were more free in other ways, too. We were allowed, for instance, when the time came for general recreation, to begin that recreation inside the house. (In the Novitiate, recreation had to begin outside the house.) Thus, we had the inestimable privilege of speaking as we changed our shoes, an unheard-of phenomenon in the Novitiate. Then, too, there were times in the Juniorate, such as Thursday and Sunday afternoons, when we could actually sit down and listen to good music, another unheard-of privilege in the Novitiate. Occasionally, too, we would put on plays for the edification of the Community. The rehearsals and other preparations for these plays gave us a great deal of enjoyment.

In general, the atmosphere of the Juniorate was not so intensely and universally spiritual throughout the day. The time we had given in the Novitiate exclusively to spiritual reading, the study of the spiritual life, instructions, and so forth, was now largely devoted to the study of the classics. Of course, we were still faithful to those

spiritual exercises which were to be practiced for the rest
of our lives: an hour's meditation daily, fifteen minutes
of spiritual reading daily, two fifteen-minute examinations
of conscience daily, and so forth. We also would make
an eight-day retreat and two three-day retreats every
year and a day of special recollection each month. Our
ideal, of course, was to offer and perform our studies in
such a way that they would be meritorious and pleasing
in the eyes of God, that they would be in reality a
constant prayer.

The Juniorate was the last place along the way where
we would all do spiritual reading (a half hour, come
to think of it) all together in the same place at the same
time. One of my friends, who is now a rather prominent
Jesuit, used to have his desk directly across the room
from mine. More often than not, he would nod and
fall asleep during spiritual reading, as all of us did,
perhaps less frequently than he. Heroically, he once
asked me to wake him should he fall asleep. This I agreed
to do. The next time he fell asleep, I took my kneeling
bench and threw it across the room at him, hitting him
in the leg. It woke him up. But he came out of the fog
as though he expected a battle. He weighed somewhere around 220 pounds and he never was fat. So
to have him come alive ready for a battle is quite a
startling experience when you happen to be the only
logical opponent in that battle. Finally he calmed down,
however, and went back to sleep — I mean back to his
spiritual reading. Later on, at recreation, I asked him
just what was the big idea, since he had asked me to
wake him and he hadn't specified the means. He informed

me wisely that he wasn't responsible when half awake. I told him to get someone else to wake him. I felt too young to die.

In the Juniorate, then, we began to appreciate two things more and more: our companions and our spiritual exercises. Each has, at times, kept us going in the right direction.

Throughout our course in the Society, the liturgy is observed as closely and dutifully as possible. But I think the Holy Week services at Florissant stand out particularly. I enjoyed them most in the Juniorate because it was there that I got more of a chance to participate. It seems that by that time we had run low on volume for the choir, so I was chosen to fill in. I forget the exact words of glowing praise that met my application for the choir, but I think it was an enthusiastic statement such as, "Maybe he'll sound all right in a crowd."

With the beauty of the lamentations and other perpetrations of the choir during Holy Week, I remember vividly the musical debut of a contemporary of mine. The choir was grouped in the sanctuary of the chapel at a solemn moment, when his turn came to sing a solo, a lamentation. The choir finished a very beautiful selection, and he picked up what he figured should be his note and began to sing. Soon he was puffing like a steam engine, because he had taken his note from the first tenors. He got through it somehow, pausing about every three words to catch his breath. Why the rest of us did not burst we'll never know. Our soloist told us later that he felt, after that session, as though he had run a mile. And he looked it.

One of the memorable events of our first Christmas in the Novitiate was being awakened for Midnight Mass, not by the bell which usually tore us rudely out of our dreams, but by a quartette of juniors singing *Adeste Fideles.*

When we were juniors, we split up into the usual quartettes to wake the community with our rather striking arrangement of *Adeste Fideles.* Most of the groups did quite well. But one group found that the notes were too high for that time of evening and ended with something that sounded like a cross between *Pagliacci* and Johnny Ray singing *Cry.* Any but a group of novices would have driven them away with a barrage of shoes. Another quartette found that their "director" had lost his voice and couldn't have produced a note with a bagpipe. So another memorable arrangement was born!

It would be wrong for me to pretend that everything in the Juniorate was undiluted bliss. For most of us, I think it was close to that. For me, it was very often a grind, chiefly because I had no real love for study, especially for the classics. I did, however, have the good fortune, or the grace, rather, to look on them as necessary means to the end I most desired in life. And at times they became somewhat interesting even for me. The vast majority of the men around me found them enjoyable, I know.

But the spirit of the Juniorate as a whole could not be beat. The joy there is in beginning, at least, to serve God, the assurance that one is on the right road, the wish to perfect oneself day by day—all these things kept us interested and alive. Our companions, all with the same

Some are quite devoted to study.

purpose as ourselves, were usually a great consolation
and help. And, where those gifted with brains enjoyed
their studies in the Juniorate, I enjoyed myself at least
once a week when I could take an ax on my shoulder
and go out and make like a North woodsman and hack
down some trees. I enjoyed, too, the sports. And there
were even times when I enjoyed praying.

Yes, the Juniorate life was a good one. At the end of
each day we recited together the Litanies of the Saints.
(These Litanies take about fifteen minutes and are

recited in all Jesuit houses once a day.) And I think that a junior in the Society of Jesus is somehow symbolized by the predicament of many juniors you would see at these Litanies: kneeling straight up, or almost straight up, sound asleep, and, more often than not, giving the responses in their sleep. I say this is symbolic of the junior, because looking back on my own Juniorate, I feel that if there was ever a time when I was asleep in the Lord, that was it!

Philosophy is an absorbing study.

IV

SOME of the houses of the New Orleans, or Southern, Province of Jesuits are quite near the Gulf of Mexico. On a certain summer day not too long ago, a Jesuit scholastic decided to go sailing. He soon found himself out farther than he had anticipated — in fact, he was not too sure just where the land had gone. World War II was going on, and he did not have to worry too much about remaining lost for any great length of time, since he was bound, sooner or later, to run into a torpedo or a mine or a submarine. Fortunately, he encountered none of these, but instead ran into the United States Coast Guard.

They picked him up and, since he certainly looked suspicious, asked him a number of questions. The first question was, of course, "Who are you?"

Without a moment's hesitation, he told them exactly who he was. "I'm a philosopher," he said, as though that explained everything. There was a moment's stunned silence. Then a sailor yelled to one of his buddies, "Hey, this guy says he's a fill-ahssifer."

After more questioning, it was finally decided that he

"I'm a philosopher."

really was a philosopher, a Jesuit scholastic studying philosophy.

In the Missouri Province of the Society, after our four years at Florissant, we go to St. Louis to begin our three-year study of philosophy. The day we left was quite an occasion, as I recall. A big yellow bus came to take us away from Florissant to our new home about twenty miles away in St. Louis. You might say there was not a dry eye in the bus. Some were wet because of the sentimental sadness of leaving the House of Bread; others, belonging to undeniable city dwellers like myself, because of joy. A four-year sojourn in the country, two of them spent on the classics, was just fine, but it satisfied. It was enough.

Our life in St. Louis really did mean a big change from our life as juniors at Florissant. In the first place, instead of wearing an insignificant little celluloid collar stuck in the necks of our cassocks, we were now allowed to wear a Roman collar just as a priest did.

The biggest difference, of course, was in our studies. We were now no longer absorbed in the classics but were engaged, rather, in the study of philosophy, a much more interesting pursuit, to my way of thinking at least. Our ideal was to gain a licentiate in philosophy, which amounted to a master's degree and which would permit us to teach philosophy. During this time, too, we studied some science and mathematics, assuredly a welcome change from a steady diet of Latin and Greek.

In the course of our three-year philosophy study, we worked on the side for our bachelor's and master's degrees in whatever courses and whatever field we chose.

Another big change was that we were now living in the city rather than isolated in the country. Quite often now we saw people who were not Jesuits. And this was really something to get used to, believe it or not.

One of the collegiate librarians asked me one day if all Jesuits were snobs. Naturally, I resented what he had said but had enough control of my voice to ask him what made him think so.

"They go right by without even speaking," he told me. "Most of them seem to be looking at the floor."

I assured him that this was not due to any snobbishness, and asked him how forthright and brave he would be around other people if he hadn't seen any, practically, for four years. He agreed, finally, that the situation might call for some adjustment. And it does.

In our day, one of the greatest delights of moving from Florissant to St. Louis came from the fact that in St. Louis each of us actually had his own room instead of having to share a loftlike dormitory with everyone else. The rooms weren't much, true, but they seemed like palaces after the dormitories and study halls of Florissant. We lived in what was known as the Pine Building, so called for the subtle reason that it bordered on Pine Street. And it had all the brilliant cleanliness possible in St. Louis. Which is to say that you could stay a lot cleaner by not brushing against the walls. But it was definitely home, and we loved it.

Another big innovation, and perhaps one of the most startling to us fledglings, was the fact that, while our philosophy courses were private, our extra courses for our degrees were taken in St. Louis University. Here we were in class with college students, many of them coeds. In one of my classes in Chaucer, for example, there were three or four of us Jesuits, two or three nuns, and twenty-six coeds. A slight change from the ocular and olfactory atmosphere of Florissant. This, also, took some getting used to.

In the city, too, our recreations were much more free. We put on and sometimes attended plays. And, after four

The examiners are kindly men, always seeking to encourage the scholastic and to draw the answers from him in a gentle manner.

years without a movie, we finally were allowed to attend movies at the university occasionally. The first two we saw, I remember, were *Brother Orchid* and *Irene*. They thrilled me as much, I think, as the first movie I had seen as a kid.

Just as there is a change in the *type* of study indulged in at St. Louis University, so the course of study at this point becomes, probably, more intensive also. The young Jesuit studies Logic, to learn and to put into practice the rules of thinking clearly and truthfully. In the study of Metaphysics, he looks into the causes of things and into the nature of existence. In Cosmology he studies the world about him and its causes. In Psychology he looks into the nature of man, and in Ethics he studies, as far as is possible from a natural viewpoint, a man's moral obligations. Finally, in Natural Theology, he learns all he can about God from natural reason.

At the end of each year, he is examined in a way quite different from the method used in the Juniorate. With a great deal of trepidation, he goes into a room where four of his teachers, now examiners, are already comfortably seated. He himself takes the teacher's desk in front of the four. Then they examine him orally and in Latin, on the courses he has finished that year. At the end of his three years of philosophy, he undergoes what is known as the *De Universa* exam, which is a comprehensive examination on everything he has studied in philosophy in the past three years. If he lives through this, he is well on the way to becoming a formed, completed Jesuit.*

As far as I was concerned, the philosophical studies had it all over those of the Junioriate. In fact, near the end of my third and final year of philosophy, I began to detect a slight flicker of interest in the stuff. With the study of Natural Theology, I began to realize how im-

---

* Actually, these exams are not as bad as they sound. One is usually ready for them and only knows a moment of panic as he enters the room. He finds that the examiners are quite human and even kind about the whole thing. After all, they went through it themselves. On the other hand, there is the rare case of the man who lets his anticipation of the dread event so unbalance him that he sees nothing but ogres in the four kindly examiners he faces. A scholastic around my time used to pass out during these exams quite regularly. It became almost a custom that one of the examiners would rush him a bottle of pop and some cookies so that he would remain conscious to the bitter end. Fortunately, most examinees come through without the need of such stimulants.

portant all this was going to be for the climax of our
studies some years later — theology. And I began to see
in the Ethics course a good preliminary study for Moral
Theology.

It is not surprising, I think, that during the intense
period of study in philosophy, one occasionally came
upon some rather odd ways of relaxing, impulses that
were acted upon sometimes before they were fully
thought out. I can remember, for example, the day that
our little Russian janitor stuck a mop under the bed of
one of the priests,* and felt something underneath the
bed. When he looked to see what it was, he immediately
dropped the mop and came out of the room screaming.
By the merest coincidence, I happened to be there to
catch him. It took us some time to convince him that
the thing under the bed was harmless, a very realistic,
stuffed lynx.

At one time, in St. Louis, we were occupied in cleaning
out what had been an old museum. So it was impossible
to predict just what sort of animal one might come upon
in the corridors. We had the lynx, of course, and then
there was a python who showed up quite frequently in
unexpected places. We also stumbled upon two realistic
busts of Molière and Racine. One morning one of these
classical gentlemen was found in a bed when the excitator** came to awaken its occupant. He had supposed
he was shaking a cold, stiff corpse.

---

* No one ever stuck a mop under a scholastic's bed except
the scholastic.
** I should explain that the excitator has the unwanted
job of waking anyone who happens to be still asleep at

Our particular group was engaged in philosophical studies during the course of World War II. We attended quite a number of lectures on air raids, first-aid procedures, and such things. One of the priests at St. Louis University took the whole thing with extreme seriousness, so that the slightest noise had him directing people to the nearest bomb shelter. One of our scholastics saw his opportunity one day and, from a fourth-floor window, laid down a walking barrage of light bulbs behind this zealous air-raid warden as he walked up the alley. The results were all anyone could have asked for.

Since we were in the city, rather than in the country, our type of exercise was necessarily a little different. Basketball, for example, had to be played on the tar patch, the asphalt-covered quadrangle outside our building. Handball was played on cement courts. So the injuries tended to be more painful than they had been on the grass at Florissant.

When we went for walks in the city, we could not just put on old clothes as we had at Florissant, but we had to dress up in our clerics, complete with black suit and Roman collar. This did not stop us, however, as there really were some beautiful places to walk in St. Louis. There was the scenic route, for example, which went up Lindell Boulevard, past some gorgeous old mansions, to Forest Park. Once we arrived at Forest Park, we were practically back in the country again except

_____

5:15 a.m. This is accomplished in different ways, depending on the stubbornness of the sleeper and the genius and strength of the excitator. Some are subtle. Most are not.

that we had had no zoo at Florissant to compare with the Forest Park Zoo.

Very often, the walks we took during our stay in St. Louis were not completely uneventful. Occasionally, for example, when we would drop in to St. Francis Xavier College Church for a visit, a little old lady who was just about always there would ask us to hear her confession. Then, when we would tell her that we were only scholastics and not able to hear confessions, she would promptly faint. She did it quite thoroughly, too. One of our scholastics, newly arrived from Florissant, very nearly fainted with her the first time he saw her in action.

Then there was the other delightful little old lady who must have lived somewhere up above Kingshighway. Whenever she spotted us, she would scream out at the top of her lungs until we were out of sight: "I KNOW YOU JESUITS! THE END JUSTIFIES THE MEANS! THE END JUSTIFIES THE MEANS!" We kept telling ourselves that this sweet little old darling with the shrill voice was undoubtedly somebody's mother.

On one occasion two of our scholastics were on an errand in downtown St. Louis. While down there, they attracted something a Roman collar never fails to attract, a drunk. With great joy and enthusiasm he greeted them as old friends and told them of his sad plight. He wanted a place to sleep and could not get a hotel room. Obligingly, the two scholastics hauled him into a cheap hotel, signed his name for him, and bade him farewell. Then they went out to get on the homeward-bound bus. Just as the bus came along, the drunk reappeared, and, as one of the scholastics stepped up into the bus, told him lugubriously, "Thanks, old pal. Thanks. Want'cha to accept a li'l token o' my esteem." And with that, he thrust something into the scholastic's astonished hands and vanished. The occupants of the bus were quite surprised to see a young clergyman standing at the front of a bus holding a half-filled fifth of whiskey. No more surprised than he was, though.

Our Thursday recreations, while not as handy as they had been out in the country, were still extremely pleasant, perhaps even more pleasant than they had been at Florissant. In our day in St. Louis, we had no villa of our own, so we used to go out into the country and wander, with our center of operations the summer home of some relatives of one of our St. Louis University priests. This home was only a short distance out of town, on the Meramec River. Each Thursday we would hop in the big yellow bus and merrily make our way countryward. It was my privilege for three years to drive this handsome bus, and no one ever discovered in that time that I was color-blind and should have had trouble with the stop lights. Come to think of it, maybe my passengers did know of my disability — they were usually so silent.

There was one spot in particular that we found extremely suitable for picnic purposes. It was a bridle path, well up above the river in the hills, and it was beautiful at all seasons of the year. I can remember Father Adrian Kochanski, another scholastic and myself setting out along the bridle path, with only ourselves and seventeen sandwiches.* We would build a fire in the middle of

---

* As I write these words, even I am tempted to think them an exaggeration. I am certain, however, of the literal truth

the bridle path and toast away and eat away, not caring if an occasional inquisitive horse did wander by to see what was going on.

Today the philosophers have acquired their own villa elsewhere. But we liked it the way it was.

There were many things to keep us amused and profitably occupied in our life in St. Louis. The scholastics helped, for example, with the Sacred Heart Program, which originates at St. Louis University. There were publications to work on: *The Historical Bulletin* and *The Modern Schoolman.* I worked for a time on the latter, until one of the book reviews I wrote was returned to me with the note, "I am afraid the publishers would eschew us were this review published." I have since published reviews of hundreds of books, most of them, probably, unfavorable, and have never been eschewed by a publisher yet. But I figured then that any organization talented enough to use a word like "eschew" had no need of my eschewable services.

There was, too, the Mission Stamp Bureau, where the scholastics collected, sorted, and sold stamps for the missions.

Then there was our choir work. Our favorite selection, in my time, was the *Tu Es Petrus,* one which allowed us really to cut loose with the vocal chords. Father Adrian Kochanski, who directed the choir, felt just as we did about it. Father Leo Sweeney, who played the organ, found our volume a challenge to his own. The first time we cut loose with this vocal orgy, it was being broadcast

here. We not only *brought* seventeen sandwiches. We ate them! Oh, there were giants in those days!

over the air. I understand that Brother Rueppel, then manager of the radio station, watching the volume indicator, first began to sweat, then to swear in a religious way, and then to pray.

We enjoyed, too, the beauty of the Holy Week ceremonies. And we were certainly not above enjoying some of the humorous things which happened during this time, incidents made more hilarious, of course, by the solemnity of the occasion and the necessity of maintaining a straight face. There was, for example, the chair which broke under one of the priests who had been sitting the whole thing out in the sanctuary with his biretta on his head all the time. Then there were the glaring mistakes which occurred in the singing and which occasionally forced half the choir to leave the public eye for the moment. There was the time when one of the priests, with an unalloyed tin ear, was murdering each individual note of a High Mass. Most of us in the choir were barely managing to keep from chuckling, when a drawl came from the first-bass section, "Wait 'til he gets to the Preface and throws caution to the winds!"

During Holy Week, too, we used to go out and help in other parishes as we were needed. Mr. Jack Scully and Mr. John Lasca went out one Holy Week to help in a parish. Since both of them are comedians, and neither is an opera star, they had great difficulty practicing the parts they had to sing together. They even had to practice in separate rooms. They figured that the pastor would be able to unify their efforts. But when they arrived at their destination, they were told that the pastor had a cold and would be unable to assist them. So they had to sing together without his sobering help. They came out only second or third best. But they did live through it somehow. We always did.

Then there were our speech classes run by Father Robert Johnston, S.J. He was able to keep things humming, largely because of the great interest and enthusiasm he himself had for his subject, and because he himself was as interesting as his classes.

As we went through our life in the Philosophate, the important thing was, of course, that we become learned men. But it was even more important, far more important, that we become holy Jesuits. And we had an obligation to strive for both learning and holiness. So it was that we kept up all the spiritual exercises we had begun to practice at Florissant: our meditation, Mass every day, our examination of conscience, our retreats and triduums, our spiritual reading, our monthly recollections. All these helped form the most important phase of our characters.

At the end of our three years of philosophical studies, we were given Minor Orders, the first steps toward our ordination to the priesthood — a goal still a long way off. And at the end of our philosophy, too, we went out to put into practice some of the things we had learned, both the spiritual and the intellectual truths.

But before describing the Jesuit's "regency," the three-year teaching period which follows his study of philosophy, I should like to philosophize a bit about summer vacations.

In the wide open spaces of Jesuit villas, there is always plenty of room to breathe freely.

V

All things have their season. . . .
[There is] A time to be born and a time to die. . . .
A time to destroy, and a time to build.
A time to weep, and a time to laugh.
A time to mourn, and a time to dance.

(Eccles. 3:1–4)

ANYONE who works steadily and with some energy at a job realizes that his efficiency will be increased if he can occasionally make a complete break from his job. In fact, after a certain time, his efficiency will decrease in direct proportion to the extent of his forcing himself to stick with a job from which he needs a vacation. This is especially true where the work is intense and uninterrupted mental work.

The Society of Jesus, like anyone with any sense, realizes that her men are going to last much longer and do their work much more efficiently if they are given a change of atmosphere whenever possible. A man who is making his way in the business or professional world or a secular student will very often find ways to give himself some sort of break, ways which are not ordinarily open to the Jesuit. The college student or the businessman can, for example, take a night off to go dancing, or he can lift his spirits reasonably with a drink or two. Then, too, he is not always bound down to the extreme regularities of life which a Jesuit observes. He can usually find at least one day, for example, when he will be able to sleep a little later. But the Jesuit rises at 5. Even though he might not realize until after breakfast at 7:15 that he is up and moving, he has actually been floundering about since 5 o'clock. There are usually one or two alert enough in each community to reassure him on this point should he ask.

It is not strange, then, that the Society sees to it that her young men in their studies are given good vacations and a complete change of scenery during the summers. At the beginning of one's Jesuit life, during the two years of Novitiate, such a complete change of scene is not thought necessary, and the novices' vacation consists largely in a change of order, with longer and more frequent recreations.

The juniors, since they are following a rather intensive schedule of studies during the year, enjoy a much better vacation. They spend the first two weeks of their summer at Charbonierre. For these two weeks, which are known as Long Order, they are not allowed to touch any book connected with their studies. (You will find an occasional unique character who would wish to do so.) After two weeks at Charbonierre, they return to the seminary, and their vacation order for the rest of the summer (from about July 5 to September 1) is known as Short Order. There is as much recreation on these days as they wish to take and think they need. They can study languages or whatever they wish but there are very few formal courses.

The vacations at Charbonierre are necessarily quite simple and even primitive. There is something that passes for a swimming pool. The dormitory accommodations are not quite up to those of the better hotels or even motels. The beds, for example, are not beds at all, but army cots. There is still no decent ball diamond at Charbonierre, and so the outfielders find themselves running up and down hills, jumping over ditches, swerving around trees, and occasionaly even scrambling up a tree should the ball be sailing in that direction.

Yet with all its simple primitiveness, Charb provides just the type of vacation a junior needs. It is a good change of scenery from his environment of the school year. He can work off much of his excess energy by chopping down as many trees as he wishes and by doing the humble work assigned him around the villa. He is, above all, away from the sight of books for at least two weeks. And this, to me at least, has always been one of the outstanding and necessary features of any vacation.

During the school year, the junior is not allowed to read novels. During his summer vacation, he can read whatever novels he can lay his hands on in the Juniorate library. This gives him a chance, not only to relax, but to begin to appreciate the classics of fiction, because the Juniorate novel collection does not include Kathleen

Windsor, but tends more toward Dickens, Thackeray, and company. For me, the Juniorate summers were real eye openers. I had read part of a book once when I was in high school, and I don't even remember the title. But it was during these summer vacations in the Juniorate that I began to realize how wonderful reading could be and I believe that I have probably averaged one book every two or three days since that time. Like many other Jesuits, I can thank the Juniorate regime for a great love of reading and for the many hours of pleasure that love has brought, for the odd, and sometimes the sleepless, moments it has filled.

Our summer vacations as philosophers were much more glamorous. But that was only natural, I believe, since the studies required more concentration, and hence our need for a change, for a real vacation, was that much greater. The philosophers' villa is in Waupaca, Wisconsin, in the heart of the dairy country. Not that we cared anything about dairies, but it was also lake and pine tree country. We were allowed to spend about six weeks of two summers at this villa.

Loyola Villa at Waupaca is in the midst of some of the most gorgeous natural sights I have ever seen. Its surroundings are thick with pine trees, so straight and tall that they seem to have been pulled up out of the ground rather than to have grown that way. The villa is on a hill overlooking Sunset Lake, one of a long chain of many lakes.

The life at Loyola Villa in Waupaca consisted largely in swimming, boating, fishing, and having picnics. Since there were so many different lakes, all of them different in temperature and surroundings, one could pretty well choose the exact type of swimming he wanted. Our lake, Sunset, was always rather warm. Long Lake, farther up the chain, was always pretty cool. Running into Long Lake was Emmens Creek, in whose spring-fed water one could turn blue in no time.

We attracted no little attention when we went out on a boat picnic. Sometimes we went in small groups of only two or three up to ten, but occasionally there would be as many as forty of us, packed into our big lifeboat, which we usually towed around with a small motorboat. At such times, people did stare at us wondering where we were being towed and for what.

On some evenings, after supper, we would put the members of our forty-voice choir into this lifeboat and tow them around the lake as they harmonized on everything from Palestrina's *Kyrie* to *Sleep, Kentucky Babe*. The people along the shore came to love these evening concerts — and missed them a great deal, they told us, when we cut them out during the war.

We had large grounds at our villa, so that plenty of softball games were going on all summer. There was also plenty of work, the kind that helped us to relax from our studies. There were trees to be cut and there was a road to be built. We had, too, our assigned work indoors, keeping the house clean and in good shape, helping in the refectory, cooking, and so forth. We even spent a miserable part of one summer painting the place, inside and out.

Our villa was certainly no mansion. The entire beauty of Loyola consists in its natural surroundings and not in any Jesuit-made buildings. There was no heat at all in the building, so that early in the summer the fireplace in the big assembly hall became extremely popular. The rooms were small and each one was shared by two men. The chapel was extremely poor. And yet, again, it was just what we needed for our summer, a complete change from the city life and the study life of St. Louis. As at every villa, we had our Long Order and Short Order. During the former, we were not allowed to touch a book. And once that two weeks was over, the amount of study was up to the individual. Many had summer courses to do to receive credit toward their degrees. Many were working on theses. But most of us saw to it that we took good advantage of all the vacation that was being offered us by the Society.

Since we knew a good number of people around the lake, not personally, perhaps, but by sight, and since they knew us, again not personally but as a group, we did have some contact with them. Two or three times each summer, for example, we brought our ball team downtown for a game of softball with a local team. The summer following my ordination, when I was stationed at Waupaca with the philosophers, I went downtown just before this game was to start. So I was sitting in the bleachers when the philosophers made their entrance. And what an entrance it was! Whoever had been in charge of transportation had not thoroughly investigated what he was getting. A huge, double-decker cattle truck, so completely enclosed that one could not see inside, backed up to the very edge of the field. I could hear the people around me, young men, young girls, old ball

Jesuits usually travel first-class.

fans, asking one another what this could be that was being delivered. Soon a ramp came down from the back of the truck onto the field, and down the ramp, with no awareness that anything out of the ordinary was taking place, calmly strolled about seventy black-panted philosophers. They acted, I must say, as though they traveled by cattle truck every day.*

---

* Since writing this and discussing it with other Jesuits, I find that this form of transportation is not too uncommon among our men. In fact, on one occasion, a rather large group of young Jesuits was transported in sweltering heat to a railroad station some twenty miles away in a closed moving van. Nor were they helped much by the fact that they were carrying their luggage and wearing black suits.

During our years of regency or teaching, we Jesuits of the Missouri Province usually go to Campion, our boarding school in Prairie du Chien, Wisconsin, for our summer villas. Since Campion is a boarding school, conditions there are much more civilized than at Waupaca. The rooms are much better, the surroundings much more finished. There are no lakes, but there is plenty of river to make up for it. There is also a golf course. And I might say that while I myself can only do one trick with a golf ball, that is, hit it so that it describes a lovely, graceful arc to the right and returns to me, there are many Jesuits who are much better than ordinary golfers. Campion is their stamping grounds.

If a scholastic teaches out west, he more than likely will go to Fraser, Colorado, for his summer villa. This is a lovely place as far as scenery is concerned. Just now, there is really nothing there but a group of not-too-large mountain cabins. But it is a nice, primitive, rugged villa and enjoyable as such. At the present writing, Father Bill Steiner is directing operations on a grand new log building which will make living at Fraser much more pleasant in the near future.

There is another villa which is not much thought of because so few are allowed to enjoy its advantages. And that is the summer "villa" we enjoyed as scholastics in Belize, British Honduras, one of the foreign missions of the Missouri Province Jesuits. The scholastics who teach in Belize have their choice of any number of such "villas." They can go to San Pedro, one of the Caribbean cayes (or islands) surrounding the colony, or they can go to a place called Orange Walk, where a very good friend of the Belize Jesuits owns a ranch. Or they can make a sort of grand tour of the entire colony of British Honduras. Since I myself had my regency in British Honduras, I was privileged to sample all such "villas" during the summer and winter vacations. And they were extremely enjoyable vacations.

The villa for the theologians of the Missouri Province of the Society is at a place called The Island. This is exactly what it claims to be, an island surrounded by Lake Beulah, a short distance from Mukwonago, Wisconsin, which is, in turn, about thirty miles from Milwaukee. Since a Jesuit is a much older and more sedentary individual by the time he reaches Beulah than he was, say, as a philosopher, Beulah is also a much more sedentary villa. Those of us who wished, however, did have our share of baseball, tennis, swimming, and fishing.

Next to our villa at Beulah is, of all things, Burr Oaks, a girls' camp. Here some seven hundred various-sized elementary school females cavort during the summer. They, too, after a while realize that our minds are on the priesthood. I can remember, however, occasions when they did not understand. Each year, for instance, we used to lend them our big red truck to help haul their baggage and perhaps some of the girls from the depot in Mukwonago to their camp. The year I was a minister (one who has charge of the temporal affairs of the villa) at The Island, they asked as usual to borrow our truck. And our superior told me that since they had no driver, I should drive it for them. So I did. On the way back from the station, two of the camp counselors rode along. As we traveled the few miles of highway to The

Furious activity characterizes the theologians' villa.

Island, one of the counselors apparently figured she was
going to be out in the sticks for a few weeks and might
as well make the acquaintance of any of the natives who
happened to be handy.

"What do you do out here all the time?" she asked.

"Like to fish, myself," I told her.

It was the first thing I thought of. I hate to fish.

We went on a few moments in silence. Then she tried again. "Well, what do you do, say, on the night of the Fourth of July?"

"Always shoot firecrackers, myself," I told her.

We didn't seem to have much conversation the rest of the way. I do hope her Fourth of July wasn't too boring.

I cannot make any reference to our life at The Island without mentioning our good friends, George and Mrs. Babl. Mr. Babl is the baker in Mukwonago and he baked for us all summer long, never charging us anything like what his wonderful baking was worth. I got to know him my first summer at Beulah, in 1947, and he has been a wonderful friend ever since. He is the type of friend without which we Jesuits would feel 90 per cent less than human beings. And it is the help and loyalty of friends like him which keep us going.

Yes, the Society treats us wonderfully, taking care of us even to the extent of invigorating summer vacations. The vacations as such end with our third year of theological studies. By that I mean there is no formal group vacation for us after that time. The significance of this is not that we stop working once we have finished our course but that we simply do not have the time to arrange for a vacation at any definite time. Again, however, let it be said that the solicitude of the Society is very nearly perfect. Any priest can, if he wishes, get away to one of the villas for a week or two of vacation. Although there are far too few of us who take advantage of this privilege, there are many who wisely do.

So, in the matter of vacations, as in all other things, the

Society of Jesus takes care of her members, at the same time charitably admitting that each one has the sense to take care of himself.

The Jesuit scholastic is a sympathetic and kindly teacher.

VI

AFTER his three years of philosophical study, the Jesuit is sent to one of the high schools of his province to teach boys. This is quite a change from anything he has experienced so far. And it is a good chance for him to put the things he has learned into practice. One of the really great men of the Society, Father William Mc-Gucken, who was for many years Prefect of Studies of the Missouri Province, once summed up perfectly the purpose of the Jesuit's period of teaching or regency. Writing for the Missouri Province *Jesuit Bulletin*, Father McGucken said:

To the Jesuit, teaching has ever been an apostolate, the classroom just as hallowed a place to win souls for Christ as the far-off mission land of India. Rightly, Jesuits can take pride in the prestige and efficiency of their schools, a prestige and efficiency purchased through self-sacrifice and a deathless enthusiasm, despite the every day monotony of classroom routine, a routine, however, that becomes a glorious adventure to Jesuits trained in the Ignatian ideal of the apostolic work of teaching. . . .

Most of all, the Society can glory in the fact that God and Christ, His Son, have always had a prominent place in her schools and universities. Her object throughout these centuries has ever been to impart truth to her students; yet she has never lost sight of the fact that there is no truth worth seeking if He who is Truth itself is ignored. *Inform*ation alone has never been the aim of the Society's schools; rather it has been the *form*ation of Christian scholars and Christian gentlemen. More than that; her aim has been, so to speak, a *transform*ation of the youth entrusted to her care into capable and energetic, Catholic American saints, even into saints and apostles, who, because of the knowledge they acquire of Christ Our Lord, will love Him and follow Him always — Christian gentlemen who will always put first things first and will regard solid and perfect virtue "of greater moment than learning or any other natural endowment."

This is the sort of job the young Jesuit steps into when he goes out to begin his three years of teaching. This is what is expected of him, to be not only a teacher, but a *Jesuit* teacher, one who will strive to instill the love he himself has of Christ into those he will teach.

Besides being a good test of his worth, regency is, for the scholastic, a welcome change after the past seven years of rather intensive study. Not that he is going to have less work to do now — on the contrary — but it is a different kind of work, in which his attention is given to others rather than to himself. After all, he has been in front of a desk for about twenty years now. It's time he looked behind one.

The regency period, too, provides good practice for the Jesuit, a good way of learning his future trade, because he really does learn how to teach by teaching. The lessons he himself learns as a teacher far surpass the number of things he is able to teach his boys.

Regency has the further advantage, I believe, of show-ing the Society whether a man is capable of teaching or not. He may be the most brilliant man in the Society and still, for some reason or other, be unable to teach. Or it may be found that he is better at teaching younger boys than older ones. Or he may be more proficient at teaching college students than high school students. Frequently enough, the Society finds that this or that scholastic could teach anybody anything under any conditions.

The time of regency is a time of rather rude awaken-ing for the scholastic. Up to now, just about all his ideas on teaching, all his ideas of zeal for others, too, have been in the order of theories and ideals. It is during his regency that he will reduce many of the theories he has to prac-tice. He will reduce many other theories, not to practice, but to the extinction which is rightfully theirs. He will discover whether the ideals he has are genuine or not.

He will perhaps have been under the impression, as he dreamed of teaching during the past few years, that no one can help listening to the truth, that if one has the truth to impart he will always have an attentive audience to hear it. He may go by that unrealistic theory that it is impossible to be dull or dry if one has the truth to offer in class. The teaching scholastic discovers the fallacy and even the absurdity of such a theory in his first week of teaching in a high school. He can be just as dull with the truth as he could be with a pack of lies. One of his biggest jobs will be, not to gather the truth (he has been doing that for many years), but to find ways of making it interesting and memorable.

**It is impossible to present the truth without arousing
great interest and enthusiasm.**

The brand new teacher very often finds that his jittery
charges seem to be most bored by the very things he
considers his best stuff. It may be dessert to him, but
it's spinach to them. They are simply not interested. Class
time for most of them is just the time they have to use
up while waiting to get back out in the yard to the
softball game. And this is what turns a man from the
theorist into a teacher, because it is up to him to get
them interested in the things which he knows are important but which seem trifling to them.

Perhaps, in the years previous to his teaching, he has envisioned large crowds of potential converts following him about. He has probably had a picture in his imagination of himself going through the school yard pursued by throngs of students, asking him to help them decide their vocations, putting questions to him about the higher realms of contemplation — in short depending upon him for all these lofty things and many others. And it is true that there probably will be a throng of boys following him or surrounding him wherever he goes. But their questions and their problems will be quite different from what he had imagined. They will be asking him where the heck is the baseball equipment or begging him to let them out of jug that night. They will be asking him to take care of a busted thumb or a nosebleed or to lend them a fountain pen because they forgot theirs today. Oh, he'll have followers all right, but he could never have dreamed of their motives for following him.

During his teaching years, naturally, the scholastic's first activity will be teaching. This he has had some little practice in, perhaps, but so little that it is negligible. He will learn to teach by going into a classroom and teaching. And, in the classroom, he will soon be able to tell whether he has prepared his matter properly or not, because there is no test comparable to the test a group of teen-age boys can give a teacher. His matter has to be presented, not just well, but terrifically well, in order to win the approval, or even the attention, of these strictest of critics.

The Jesuit scholastic soon finds that there is much more to teaching than just going into a classroom. He has to repeat and repeat and repeat even the simplest things. He has to be prepared thoroughly for each class. He has to test frequently, as often as every day, to see if they're getting what he's putting out. He has to correct thousands on thousands of papers, homework, and examinations. He has to keep his class on its toes by interesting variations and by a constant flow of questions. He must be, at first at least, a very rigid disciplinarian. Before beginning our regency, we were told by Father Mc-Gucken, "Don't smile at them until Christmas." And Father Henry Sullivan, principal at Creighton Prep in Omaha for twenty-five years, added in his own inimitable way: "When they go home for Christmas vacation, you can pat them on the head and say 'Merry Christmas.' But don't overdo it." There is a reason for this. A few months of rigid discipline and the rest of the year will be completely enjoyable and profitable for both teacher and students. The temptation, of course, is to do just the opposite because the lads are so likable right at first. What the teacher must realize is that, likable as they are, in those first months they are judging him and unconsciously figuring how much they'll be able to get by with later on. They are naturally on their best behavior for that time, like the ball club that is "playing over its head."

So the scholastic teacher has to become somewhat of a universal genius.

Besides his teaching, the scholastic will have a great deal of prefecting to do. He will be watching over boys in study halls. He will be checking their attendance at various things, such as daily Mass. He will be supervising their games during the day and the social functions, fun nights, and dances that they participate in outside of school time. Here, again, he will soon develop a facility, an uncanny sort of intuition for being in the right place even ahead of the right time. Those who do not develop this ability never really become successful prefects. Actually, it is neither uncanny nor intuition, but only the unconscious or implicit efficiency that comes from experience.

Sometimes, it will seem to the teaching scholastic that he has more to do outside of class than in class. And it is true that he will be involved in a great number of extracurricular activities. Jesuits believe heartily in such things for their boys, because it is in them that the students can put into practice the things they are learning. The scholastic might find himself coaching a basketball or a football team. He very frequently finds himself the moderator of a sodality or of a speech group. He will be called on to moderate the school paper or yearbook. There may come a time during the year when he will be asked to produce a play. Or he might be in charge of any one of a number of clubs: a literary club, a library club, or some athletic club. I recall the night, during my own regency, when the superior called me in and asked me if I knew anything about credit unions. Naturally, I told him I had no idea of what they were all about. Whereupon he informed me that it would be advisable to find out what they were all about since I would be organizing one within a week or so.

The scholastic is certain, then, to find himself involved in many and varied activities. And it is here that he comes to know the boys better and to be better able to help them. It is here especially that he will prove how well he is able to reduce theory to practice.

The scholastic finds himself involved, too, in plenty of manual and menial work. Boys are not young ladies and are not blessed or cursed with their neatness.* So the scholastic will find himself time and time again cleaning up classrooms, straightening out clubrooms, and, in general, removing the traces of the marching armies we enroll in our high schools. He will find himself checking and storing and even washing athletic equipment and other equipment used around the school. He will find, too, that his superiors will, on rare occasions, have to call on him to help out around the house. And the Society watches closely to see how he handles himself in such humble duties.

He will often find himself involved in situations where he will be tempted to laugh but doesn't dare. He may occasionally find a freshman imprisoned in one of the lockers and he must have a straight face by the time he lets him out. He will find many of the misdemeanors committed by his boys so humorous that it will be almost impossible to bawl them out with a straight face, but he must do it. He can't even relent because he himself might have once done the same thing. He might even find himself doling out a punishment he was once given himself.

---

* I reread these words with trepidation. I have known those in charge of girls' schools who have claimed they could never figure how young ladies could look so neat and leave a room or a whole school looking so sloppy.

He will discover, after a while, one very consoling thing about his regency. He will find that his influence and example are having a much greater effect on the boys under his care than he had realized. They will look to him for a great deal of casual, offhand, almost implicit advice. He will discover that boys with vocations have, perhaps, begun to think along those lines because they respected him so much when they were freshmen. He will probably not realize until years later, as a priest, that his influence was strongly felt by the boys around him, even though neither he nor they realized it at the time.

Yes, the teaching years are a maze of activity. The scholastic is on the go from early morning until late at night. And yet, with all this activity, his essential spiritual exercises must go on as usual. He goes to Mass and Holy Communion every day. He makes an hour's meditation every day. He examines his conscience twice every day. He prepares his morning's meditation for fifteen minutes every night. The Society of Jesus knows that it is somewhat more difficult for him now to fit in all his spiritual exercises. But she knows, too, that it is by no means impossible. She knows that if he is remiss in these things now, he will be just as remiss later on as a priest. The Society does not censure men because they are weak as teachers or weak as disciplinarians, but rather finds the proper spot to use their talents. But she does watch very carefully their faithfulness or the lack of it in keeping up their spiritual exercises. Regency is a time of probation, a test for the young Jesuit, and he does not pass that test just by being a good teacher. He passes it in proportion to his obedience, his genuine humility, his respect for authority no matter how annoying that authority might sometimes be from a natural viewpoint, and the amount of genuine spirituality that he shows. This is what counts most in the Jesuit's character. And this is what the Society is watching for most closely.

It is a trying time, then, this period of regency, and yet it is also a very happy and satisfying time for the scholastic. It is his first chance to exercise his zeal directly. There is a great thrill in being able to teach, to impart knowledge to others. And it is thrilling, too, to discover the wonderful character that lies beneath the helter-skelter and deceptive exterior of a boy. The literary essay, "What Is a Boy?" says that a boy is truth with dirt on his face. But a boy is much more than that. He is truth and goodness and an image of God. And on his face is a lot more than dirt.

To give the clearest idea of what regency is like for a Jesuit scholastic, it would be best, perhaps, to go through some details of my own regency. There is one disadvantage to this, and that is that I did not teach in an American school but had the rare privilege of being sent as a scholastic to teach at St. John's College, our school in Belize, British Honduras, in Central America. Truly, a book could be written about those three years. But I will confine myself only to what a scholastic's life was like in general. And, for the most part, it was much the same as the life of a teaching scholastic in the United States.

A typical day for a Jesuit scholastic in Belize went

something like this: At 5:30 every morning we had Mass for ourselves. (Naturally, this presumed that one was out of bed and ambulatory, even if not fully awake.) Between 6 and 7 a.m., I would check attendance of the college boys at two Masses in the cathedral. At 7 o'clock I had breakfast, and at 7:20 I was back at the cathedral herding the boys inside for another Mass. This Mass ended early enough to permit class to start at 8 o'clock, and classes were from 8 to 12 every day. At 12 o'clock, we would get something to eat, and I would spend the rest of the time until 3 o'clock repairing and getting in shape our athletic equipment, basketballs, soccer balls, baseballs, cricket balls, goal posts, basketball uniforms, and just about everything else. From 3 until 4:30 we would prefect two yards, a field about two miles away where the boys played soccer, and the gym. Usually there were only two or three of us to watch these four places. Some trick! Prefecting the yards meant not only supervising our own boys but kicking out strangers who wandered in who had no business there. Sometimes they had to be reminded that they were unwelcome and for this purpose various technics according to age, size, and sex were employed. At 5:30 I would again get something to eat and then, much of the time, have play practice from 6 to 7 in the evening. Since our boys were in study hall from 6 to 9 each night, I had some more prefecting, this time in the study hall from 8 to 9 at night. From 9 o'clock on, I was free to perform my spiritual exercises, prepare for class, correct papers, and prepare for any other extracurricular activities demanding attention. It was our custom, too, in Belize, to listen to the American news on the radio at 10 o'clock and then stick around for a little recreation. It was good to sit around and relax for a few minutes at the end of the day with one's companions.

Our teaching schedule, too, was quite broad. I, for example, taught third- and fourth-year Latin, third- and fourth-year English and speech, second-year Arithmetic, Algebra, Geometry, and English, first-year Spanish, and Prep Geography. In third and fourth years, in our particular setup, Latin and English courses were changed each year, so that the teacher never repeated the same thing he had taught the year before. One year he would teach Livy, the next year Cicero's *Letters*, and so forth. It was really a liberal education for the teacher.

Numerous extracurricular activities also cut into our time. There were plays and entertainments, "fun nights,"* and sometimes dances. We published a monthly news magazine, which at times reached the size of thirty-six pages. There were certain annual events to prepare for, such as graduation and scholarship reports and samples or specimens of what our incipient geniuses had accomplished to date to be shown the parents. There was the annual field day, which took several weeks' preparation and which the entire city attended. There was, in short, enough to keep a man busy.

Regency in Belize was, perhaps, the happiest period I, for one, have ever known. This was due largely to the wonderful Jesuit community there, with their great char-

---

* A "fun night" is an orgy enjoyed immensely by our otherwise dignified students and no fun at all for the scholastics.

ity. I would like to mention each one of them, but obviously cannot. I must, however, mention with gratitude Bishop David Hickey, who was my superior for three years there, and who was completely fair, human, and inspiring at the same time.

I made many friends there who are still very close to me even though a great distance separates us. Among them are Eric Russell, Nacho Valdes, Edgar Gegg, and Lee Anderson. They are not only great friends but, I think, great men as well.

We had our share of recreation, too, in Belize, during vacations and, when we could snatch the time — which wasn't very often — on week ends. We knew the thrill of sailing and fishing and swimming in the Caribbean. During the summer, as I mentioned in the previous chapter, we spent two or three weeks at one of the cayes (or islands), at San Pedro, about thirty miles north of Belize, or at a ranch at Orange Walk. Occasionally, too, in the summer, we visited the bush missions where some native diocesan priests and the Jesuit fathers do heroic work. Just how heroic it was, it was good for us to discover during the summer. I can still picture my good friend, Father Phil Pick, going up-country in a new army truck which was luckily equipped with an open turret. I say "luckily" because Father Phil is a very tall man and in order to be comfortable he had to stick his head out of the turret.

Teaching in Belize was a rare experience; but regency anywhere is a rare experience. It is one of the most important parts of the young Jesuit's training, so much so that he will not be admitted to the study of theology until he has given satisfaction in his regency. And the satisfaction comes, not from his great success as a teacher, but from his humble obedience, his faithfulness as a Jesuit.

The life of serene and untroubled contemplation
deepens during regency.

The Jesuit makes a promise. . .

VII

AS I rode a rather sluggish train through the easygoing South, on my way home from Belize after three years of regency, I looked around at everything the United States had to show, as though it were all new to me. The scenery outside the train window was so much different from anything outside the country that I couldn't believe it was true. And, of course, the people looked different, too. Without detracting in any way from the wonderful people of British Honduras, I must say my own American countrymen looked great to me. At one stage of the journey, I found myself sitting across from a young lady and a young man about my age, who were deep in discussion. It seemed that the young man was a full-fledged minister and that his companion was curious about his course of studies.

"How long must you study to become a minister?" she asked.

"It takes us four years," he told her. "After our other schooling, of course."

"Other schooling?" she asked him.

"Oh yes. We must have finished high school before we begin our ministerial studies."

He then noticed my Roman collar and what I imagine was my relative youth at the time (I was nearing my twenty-ninth birthday), and asked me, "And how long do you have to study?"

"Fifteen years," I told him. "Thirteen before ordination and two after."

The young lady was properly shocked. "Fifteen years!" she exclaimed. "Doesn't that seem an awfully long time?"

I didn't mean to be abrupt, but I was tired from my trip. "I really don't know," I told her wearily. "I've only finished ten of them."

They left me soon after that. We had no occasion to add to the conversation.

It is true that it takes fifteen years to hatch out a Jesuit. Two years of Novitiate, two of Juniorate, three years of philosophy, three years of teaching, four years of theology, and a final year called "Tertianship." But I would be willing to bet against all comers that it is the fastest fifteen-year training in existence. One reason for this is, of course, that it is so well broken up into different and varying stages. But the main reason probably is that when one has a definite purpose in mind and sees the necessity for every bit of training in order to attain that purpose, he does not find that the time he uses is long or seemingly wasted. On the contrary, there are times when he is uneasily aware that he simply cannot cover all he would wish to cover in the course of his preparation.

The course of training in the Society seems to me at

this time, as I look back upon it, to be as intellectually efficient as possible. And though we may err from time to time in overemphasizing or de-emphasizing the intellectual element in our lives, much as some colleges overstress or understress athletics periodically, the balance is usually pretty well preserved. In the Novitiate, the young Jesuit lays a foundation, a two-year foundation, of a future spiritual life that is to last to his deathbed. Having laid this foundation, he begins to build an intellectual structure upon it. In the Juniorate, he concentrates upon the classics, upon languages and the arts. In the Philosophate, he adds another story to the structure, by studying causes, the what and the why of things. Having absorbed two years of spiritual training and five years of more intellectual training, he is given a three-year period to let all he has learned so far sink in and settle and to see if he can make use of what he has put together so far. Having spent three years doing this, he takes up the final stage and the culmination of all his studies, around which everything else centers: the study of theology. It is during this period that he sees the reason for having studied everything that went before and that he establishes in his own mind more solid reasons for his faith and for his very vocation. Indeed, I am convinced that most Jesuits really see for the first time during theology the tremendous thing that their vocation is. And it is also here for the first time, perhaps, that his vocation gains enormous strength and greater clarity.

Besides being intellectually efficient, the Jesuit course of study is also psychologically perfect. The young Jesuit lives much like a monk in the Novitiate and not a whole

lot differently in the Juniorate. For him there are now
two worlds: that of his religious life and the one he
refers to, in quotation marks, as "the world," the one he
has forsaken. But in the Juniorate he does take one small
step toward going back into the world he has left, with
the spirituality he has accumulated in the Novitiate. He
is more free and his mind is absorbed, not with spiritual
things at every moment, but, for a great part of the day,
with his studies. He takes another step and a longer one
back into the world when he leaves Florissant to go in
to St. Louis University for the study of philosophy. Here,
he walks once-familiar streets, sees again a well-known
sky line, and meets once more his former acquaintances.
But there is a difference. By this time he has been trained
very intensely in spiritual things, and the surroundings
he has left no longer claim him. His relation now to his
former world is to be one of giving not of taking. It
takes him a little while to get used to it again, with his
new attitude toward it and, incidentally, its new attitude
toward him. But he gradually begins to do so.

Then, when he goes out teaching, he is not only in the
midst of his former sort of surroundings but is working
and teaching in the midst of them. He is no longer in a
monastic atmosphere. His life is much more free now than
it was when he was a philosopher, and he must, by this
time, have overcome whatever shyness he had toward
the world. As a regent, he is practicing the Jesuit life of
giving back what he has been taught, of letting his interior
life flow over into the exterior apostolate. After his teaching, he goes back to theology to add the final touches to
his training and to be ordained a priest, so that he can

not only teach others but help to sanctify them as well, with the sacraments and with all the powers Christ has vested in His priests.

The entire course of study — each stage of it — provides some sort of trial for the Jesuit. And included in each stage are various trials within trials. These are known as "probations."

The whole Novitiate is a period during which the young man must be tested, in order to determine whether he will be able to be a Jesuit or not. That is one of its purposes. During the Novitiate, many probations or trials are given to prepare him for his future Jesuit life and to see to it that none of the difficulties that will later face him are exactly hidden from his eyes. He is tried in humility, to see if he will be humble enough in his future life as a Jesuit. For this training, various means are used, such as the menial jobs he is given around the house — washing dishes, sweeping floors, and so forth. There is, at present, what is called a hospital probation, during which time the novices spend some time in a poor hospital, performing humble tasks for the sick. The long thirty-day retreat is another probation, to try a person's ability to acquire the spirituality necessary for successful living of the Jesuit life. The novice is also sent to live for a month among the brothers, doing, with them, the same work they do. He will know, during this trial, just how much humility he really has.

In general, the Novitiate is *the* time of trial. At the end of the Novitiate, one pronounces perpetual vows. Some will have thought things over by this time and decided that this life is not for them. Occasionally, the Society will decide that a certain candidate is unsuited for her life. But, if both the novice and the Society are reasonably sure of his fitness, he is allowed to pronounce his perpetual vows.

There is, however, the exceptional case of one who is deceived in his Novitiate for one reason or another, who considered himself fit and willing to live the Jesuit life forever, only to find, perhaps in the Juniorate, and more often in the Philosophate, that this life is not for him, that he has made a mistake. In this case, after the Society has examined the case and has seen that he really has made a mistake, that this life is not for him, and that he will be much safer in another vocation, a dispensation from his vows can be and is procured. Fortunately, such cases are relatively rare. More of those who leave do so from the Novitiate than from any other stage of the Society's training. Still, some do depart between the end of the Novitiate and ordination. It would be very surprising were it otherwise. We are not infallible, nor are the Society's superiors infallible.

Again, the teaching years, while enjoyable, are a period of trial or probation for the young Jesuit. He may find, as he practices the teaching work of the Society, that he did make a mistake and that this work is not for him. He may, of course, find that the call of the world he has left is too strong for him to resist safely. In this case, he will be dispensed from his vows. There is the extremely rare case where the Society finds that he is not fitted for her work or her life and then he will be asked to try another sort of life.

Even during the study of theology, there are some who

decide that the Jesuit life is not for them. Even after twelve or thirteen years in the Society, there are some who, immediately before ordination, decide not to go on. And it is a wise thing, even then, if one decides this way, after the right amount of thought, prayer, and advice, to act upon it. One can be dispensed even from perpetual vows, but one cannot be dispensed from the priesthood and its obligations. I do not know the rate of occurrence of such cases, but from what I do know of them, I would say there is about one every two or three years in the Missouri Province.

Still more rarely, a Jesuit priest will find the obedience or regularity or some other such obligation of the Society unsuited to his temperament, and will decide to leave to live the life of a diocesan priest. Then, as before, he will be dispensed from his vows without any stigma attached and will take up the life of a secular priest under a bishop. Again, this is a rare occurrence.

Even more rare, thank God, is the case of the priest who decides to desert his priesthood. The priesthood cannot, of course, be deserted nor dispensed from, and all we can do for those who try it is pray for their souls. Fortunately, there may be only one case like this in a generation. It is too bad that there are any at all, but we can't make over human nature or the law of averages.

Why is it, human nature being what it is and our life being as difficult for human nature as it is, that most of us persevere, keep going in what might be called an unnatural sort of life? None of us can give an adequate answer to that question, except that we know that this is our life, our vocation, to which we have been called, and that, though there are sometimes severe temptations, it is worth any struggle, any sacrifice of our natural desires, to resist them and to persevere in the life we have chosen. We know, above all, that by ourselves we would never be able to make it. But we realize that, helping us at every moment, is the grace of God, which keeps us on the right track and protects us from things that would otherwise be too much for us. Everybody has to sacrifice *some* natural elements to achieve his supernatural goal anyhow.

Why is it, though, that there are some who do not persevere but who leave the Society in the course of their studies? I am certain that I could never exhaust the reasons for their leaving. The reason is never made public, for one thing, but can only be guessed at. There are, however, certain fundamental reasons which are, I am sure, generically at least, behind a man's deciding that he does not want to live the Jesuit life any longer.

There could be, for example, certain difficulties to the Jesuit life which would become insurmountable if one allowed them to become so. By this I mean simply that the ordinary Jesuit, living his ordinary life, does not let small difficulties prey upon his mind. But the person who is wavering in his vocation, who begins to think that he is in the wrong spot, will allow the minor difficulties he encounters to become enlarged in his mind until they are insurmountable. For example, since all of us are human beings, there will be those in large communities with whom we get along less easily than with others. For most of us, this is an expected, ordinary thing, and a very minor annoyance. And we do get along with everyone, even though there is an occasional minor misunderstanding. We realize that we cannot like everyone to the same degree and we accept this fact. But for the man who is beginning to look outside of his vocation, these minor irritations and small clashes of wills will become afflicted with elephantiasis. It will then be very difficult for him to continue to live a community life.

This is not a phenomenon peculiar to the Society or to the religious life. The same thing happens to a couple who allow their marriage to become sour. Characteristics in each other which they once thought particularly lovable can become sources of great annoyance. It is not hard to become "incompatible" once the situation reaches this stage.

Second, there is the possibility that, for some, an unforeseen monotony will seem to rule their lives. I imagine that there are times in every life — that of the businessman, the professional man, the secretary, anyone — when monotony has to be overcome. It seems to me, for instance, that my own life is filled with the greatest variety while the life of a dentist is filled with the worst possible monotony. I imagine there are dentists who are of an exactly opposite opinion, otherwise there wouldn't be any dentists. At any rate, I am sure that everyone feels the touch of monotony occasionally. And it is quite possible that a Jesuit could begin to think that the life is too monotonous for him. Once this idea becomes planted, of course, he can read monotony into a great number of things where perhaps it does not really exist at all.

There is a much more valid reason than these, I am sure, why men do not persevere in the Jesuit course of

study. They discover, for some reason or other, that this
is simply not their life. They feel, perhaps, that they are
so constituted that they will not be able safely to live
the celibate life of a priest. And then it is far better for
them to leave, once they are sure. It has been argued
over and over again whether or not there is such a thing
as a temporary vocation. In my mind, there is no argument. Because we know for sure, first, that a man should
profit a great deal by even a short period of training in the
religious life, and, second, that no dispensation would be
granted were it wrong to leave the religious life under
certain conditions. To my mind, there is definitely room
in God's marvelous providence for such a thing as a
temporary vocation. And I am sure that there is many
a fine layman in the world today who is equally or even
more convinced of it than I.*

I feel sure, too, that the temptation to leave the Society
has hit most of us from time to time before our ordination. We would not be human beings if it hadn't. Temptation, in this matter, is certainly no disgrace, nor is it ever.
It is simply something to be reckoned with. It is quite
natural that in the course of our studies we should be
tempted to give up. Because it is natural for a man, first
of all, to wish to live in the married state, with a wife,
children, and a home of his own. It is natural for a man
to want his own business, his own money, his own car.
It is natural, above all, for a man to do his own will rather
than submit that will in obedience, which demands such

---

* There are, of course, those who may have lost their vocations culpably, through a lack of co-operation with the graces
given them.

great faith. All these things are natural, so it is neither surprising nor disgraceful to be tempted to want to have them, even after we have voluntarily given them up. What is important is that we be able to distinguish between a temptation — which is nothing more than the illusion that the grass is greener on the other side when we don't really need grass anyhow — and God's good providence. This is not difficult with the aid of two things: God's grace and ordinary common sense. Thank God that, normally, both are dispensed in sufficient quantities.

Since the temptations the young man encounters on his way to becoming a Jesuit priest are to perfectly good and natural things, things legitimate and praiseworthy in themselves, such as marriage, if he is to remain a Jesuit, his motive must be very lofty. And for those of us who have persevered (the vast majority of those who began), our Jesuit life is for us the greatest life possible, so that any concern with any other life is utterly out of the question. For any of us there is not the slightest desire to become President of the United States, a great business-man, a great anything — even a monsignor. For us to wish for those things would be ridiculous, because we have chosen by faith a life that we know to be eminently worth while and, for us, above any other state of life. We have taken Christ at His word when He said that He would give us a hundredfold even in this life if we would give up everything to follow Him. And we know He wasn't kidding. We know the indescribable joy that comes from knowing, loving, and trying to serve God to the best of our ability. We know the joy there is in the companionship of those who are trying to achieve that same end. None of us can describe that joy. But each of us is ever grateful to God for exposing us to it. Each of us knows how unworthy he is of such a privilege. And with that realization comes an even greater appreciation of our privilege. We know how infinitely much we are being given. And that, of course, is our safety and our salvation.

. . . and, with God's help, keeps it for life.

Theology holds the interest of one and all.

VIII

THE Jesuit scholastic, returning from his regency, often sounds like one of the original disciples returning from his first missionary trip. "Lord," the disciple said in his enthusiasm, "even the devils are subject to us in Thy name."* For a year or so after his return from teaching, during his first year of theology, about all the scholastic wants to discuss with his friends is his teaching days, the success he has had, the amount of work he had to do, and how pleasing the work was. In fact, most of us probably made ourselves obnoxious to one another more than once, with our boasting about the schools we had become so much a part of.

It is a strange feeling for the Jesuit to be back on the other side of the desk when he first comes to theology. In the Missouri Province of the Society, the Jesuit theologians study at St. Mary's College, St. Marys, Kansas. So the scholastic is again relatively out in the country. For at least three years, he has been on the teacher's side of

---

* This is not intended as any direct reference to the boys we teach in our schools but is meant simply as an indication of the teaching scholastic's enthusiasm.

the desk, pounding the matter into reluctant heads, but now he himself has to attend class and listen. Sometimes, he begins to suspect just what the boys he taught had to go through with him as a teacher.

Part way through our first year of theology a strange thing happened to me. For the first time in my life I began to enjoy studying, not so much for itself as for the tremendous interest that I discovered in the study of theology itself.

One reason was, of course, that our theological faculty at St. Mary's was composed of men who were as helpful and considerate as they were competent and able to teach their subjects with contagious enthusiasm.

The main reason for a growing attraction to the study of theology, however, was probably the fact that theology is the culmination of our course of study, that to which all other studies are ordered, and without which the others simply do not make sense. Theology is really the study of God, of what He has told men about Himself and about His world. It is the study of Christ the Son of God, and of His Church. It is also the study of God's laws, the norms that men must follow if they are to get back to God, where they belong.

We began our study of theology by looking at Scripture, at the truths which God Himself has revealed to men. We studied the prophecies about the coming of Christ and the claims which Christ made that He was the Messias and God. Following up the teachings we found in Scripture, we saw that Christ established a Church which we could recognize by four signs: it would be one, holy, universal, and apostolic.

We studied God, as one in Himself and as He really exists, three Persons in the Blessed Trinity. We studied the life and death of Christ, and we studied as much as we could about His mother, Mary. We studied the creation of the world and of men, and learned how God first elevated man to a very lofty state where he remained until Adam and Eve kicked the props out from under themselves. We saw that God helped us in our struggle to get back to Him in heaven by His grace, and we tried to find out just what His grace really is. We discovered that we get God's grace in two ways, by prayer and the sacraments. And we studied the sacraments, finding out why we knew what we did about them.

Besides looking at the nature of God and learning all we could about Him, we also looked at man in relation to God. In Moral Theology, we studied the rules that God had laid down for us. We saw that these rules had to be observed if men were to consider themselves friends of God.

We studied Scripture rather intensively for two years, both the Old and the New Testaments. Our Scripture and Hebrew studies were made memorable and fascinating by the teaching of Father Michael Gruenthaner.

On the side, we had the usual accumulation of courses along with our regular theological studies: Ascetical and Mystical Theology, in which we learned much about prayer and the upper reaches of the spiritual life; Pastoral Theology, a course designed to prepare us to meet the difficulties we would be confronted with as confessors; Archaeology and Church History.

With us still were the *toni* or speech classes we had been subjected to once every week since our earliest days in the Society. During the course of our theology, we again had to give sermons in the refectory while the rest of the community ate dinner. It was the same old story as before, except that now that we were older and had heard a great number of sermons, we were not too easy to impress. During one of my own sparkling sermons in the refectory, my good friend, Father Gene Korth, who was serving table, wheeled his serving cart directly underneath the pulpit, parked it, and casually leaned against a pillar watching me intently as I delivered my sermon. This, of course, was quite unusual since nobody ever paid any attention to a sermon unless the speaker made a mistake, in which case every head in the refectory jerked away from the food momentarily, to turn toward the preacher.

Since at the end of our third year of theology we would be ordained as priests, one of our most important courses during the third year was that of Rites, in which we learned the ceremonies of the Mass, how to administer the sacraments, and, in general, how to perform the duties of a priest.

Although our work in Rites class was quite serious, considering the dignity and importance of the things we were learning, there were occasional situations which were at least incongruous. On one occasion my friend Father Urban Kramer, now Superior of the Honduras missions in Central America, was helping another future priest, Father Ed Laskowski, to practice infant Baptism. We used for this purpose a very lifelike doll. Father

Kramer was the sponsor and was, therefore, holding the doll. Since he has hands which resemble baskets anyway, he was holding the "baby" in one of them, and not in the prescribed manner for baby holding, but by the head. Thus he could turn the "child" merely by twisting the head. I'm sure that he discovered early in his ministry as a priest that the real article is a little less pliable and yells more than our doll did.

With us, too, were the ever present examinations. Yearly, we had our oral exams, in Latin as always, with the same seemingly grim four examiners grilling us mercilessly. Besides the yearly exams, we had a couple of special exams. One was called the *"Ad Auds,"* the Latin name for the exam which qualifies the future priest to hear confessions. Since the examiners were all priests, they went to great lengths to invent ingenious and unheard-of cases to ask us in this exam, because not even in an examination would one of them take the slightest risk of touching the seal of confession. Father Gruenthaner, of course, used to enjoy himself no end by dreaming up ways and means of embarrassing and putting the examinee on the spot. On one occasion, for instance, when the poor trembling young man was scarcely seated, Father Gruenthaner, proceeding up the aisle toward him, suddenly fell down. Then he looked up and told the startled Jesuit that he had just died in the confessional and he wanted to know what the confessor should do. The "confessor" almost died himself.

The final examination in theology, an exam to end all exams, takes two hours, is all in Latin as usual, and includes all the philosophy and theology the Jesuit has studied. It has only one virtue: it is the last one.

I cannot finish speaking about exams without mentioning the remark that Father Frank Furlong, now rector at St. Mary's, made to me after my first theology exam. I had studied very hard for it and had been as scared as usual before and during the exam. At its conclusion, Father Furlong merely looked at me, shook his head, and said, "Nice try!" Nothing encourages like encouragement.

We had several hobbies, if you wish to call them that, which helped us to relax at St. Mary's. Many of us wrote articles for magazines and I wrote a couple of books as well during this time, one on theology, unpublished to date, and another, a detective story, published in 1950. The relative success of these two books, is, I hope, no indication of the successful and unsuccessful sides of my personality.*

Many of us were kept busy by The Catholic Review Service, a syndicated book review service used by a number of newspapers throughout the country.

We produced plays for the community at various more important times of the year, such as Christmas and Easter. One of the most memorable farces I have seen was not

---

* I am sure, however, that some sharper will discover, not only that I have a detective story in my past but that, at the age of fourteen or fifteen I applied for the F.B.I. And he will undoubtedly conclude that my temperament was thus predisposed for formation as a Jesuit. Be that as it may, I would like to go on record as stating that I did not join the Jesuits because Mr. J. Edgar Hoover told me (in a very nice way) that I would not be acceptable for his organization for some years.

a play at all, but a single act put on by one of the
scholastics. Father John Driscoll, of the New Orleans
Province, came into the recreation room, where everyone
was assembled one particular evening during the Christmas holidays. He was dressed, not as a Jesuit, but as a
nun. He seated himself at a table in front of the
room and, as Mother Superior, gave the "nuns" an ex-
hortation, the main theme of which was that they should
turn in their ready-made cigarettes to Mother Superior
and observe the rule of rolling their own. The irony in
the act came from the fact that scholastics at St. Mary's
were not given cigarettes but could roll their own if
they were able and so desired. Father Driscoll, a huge
man with a great jaw and tremendous hands, resembled
any given nun about as much as Primo Carnera resembles
Lily Pons.

We also managed to distract ourselves occasionally
by going out to help the pastors in various parishes in
Kansas. When we were scholastics, these occasions were
very few — Christmas and Easter, perhaps. But as priests,
since we were ordained after our third year of theology
and still had a fourth year to go, we did get to go out
fairly often to help in parishes, maybe once every month
or two, and always at Christmas and Holy Week. This
was a good chance to exercise what we had learned in
theology and a good zealous distraction as well.

The theologians at St. Mary's have always formed a
pleasingly cosmopolitan group. Although St. Mary's is
in the Missouri Province, the Southern or New Orleans
Province also sends its men to study there. In our time
there was a handful of Mexican Jesuits, and one or two

from Brazil. We also boasted at St. Mary's of one Maltese, Father Salvino Darmanin, who had bounced from one concentration camp to another during the war. We used to interview him regularly, asking which he preferred, St. Mary's or the concentration camp. And though he pointed out many advantages to the concentration camp, he did flourish at St. Mary's.

Naturally, no American is going to pass up every single opportunity he has for pulling a foreign leg or so. I recall one evening when Father Gaspar Dutra from Brazil walked into his room, turned on his lights, and began to scream like mad. On the bed lay a horrible-looking black figure, its face the shade of death. The figure was merely Father Charlie Prendergast lying in the dark, with one of those horrible rubber masks over his face. The results were highly satisfactory.

At another time, when Father Prendergast and I were walking from the scholastics' building at St. Mary's down to the main building to attend a movie, we happened to notice that behind us were Father Dutra and Father Martinez from Mexico. It was their first movie at St. Mary's, and they had no idea where it was being shown. They were following us to see where we went, so without looking back, we took them on quite a tour of the buildings. We went through the refectory, through the kitchen, out into the back yard, past the laundry, in another door, up through an old dormitory, until finally we were cornered and our two shadows discovered at last that we had been leading them astray. Then we went to the movie together.

St. Mary's itself is a fairly attractive place. We were

again out in the country, but it did seem an ideal setting in which to study about God. The food we had was good enough during our time. But there had been periods, during times of national crises when the food had been anything but satisfactory. Now, in the Society there are certain rare occasions when one can practice the virtue of humility by accusing himself of certain faults before others. It is a wonderful thing and a great opportunity, if only a small one, to practice a little of the humility of Christ. And this is the general Jesuit attitude toward the custom. Sometimes, however, it will happen that this practice can become the vehicle for a little irony, whether intentional or not. There was, for instance, the occasion during the food shortage, when one of the scholastics accused himself of three things: of speaking in times of silence without permission or necessity, of staying up late at night without permission or necessity, and of eating out of the accustomed times without permission. It took a while for the subtle significance of this one to penetrate.°

Again, at St. Mary's the "collectors" popped up. One of the scholastics ran screaming out of the shower one day because what he had thought a section of hose coiled up in a corner turned out to be alive. He had been perfectly willing to share the shower with a hose. White rats, squirrels, all kinds of animals, were collected, but the most likable of these characters was, I believe,

___

° This recalls that other classic — the irony of which was completely unintentional, I am sure — of the scholastic who accused himself of making an ass of himself by imitating superiors.

*One never knew when he would encounter one of the lovable
and well-trained pets with which St. Mary's abounded.*

the pet racoon owned by Father Gene Coomes. He
(the coon) finally got a bit too disrespectful to have
around, even to the extent of taking a halfhearted nibble
at the leg of one of our superiors on one occasion.

Then there was Father Walt Harris' pet kitten, which
bore the proud name of Clancy. By an odd coincidence,
one of our superiors bore the same proud name.

No one could speak or write of St. Mary's College
without mentioning one of the institutions there, a man
who will always be young, John Homan. John has been

working for the Jesuits at St. Mary's for over twenty-five years. He has learned to know so many of them that he can imitate any given one at any given moment, and he does so. John is especially in his glory at the beginning of each year when the new theologians arrive at St. Mary's, strangers to the place and to him as well. He enjoys telling them that maybe this year he will get to be ordained although his ordination has already been put off for twenty-five years. It takes some time for them to discover that he is our Number One workman.

Others will ask John, as they see him working about the halls, if he is a brother. He will always reply without any hesitation and with perfect truth, "No, I am a father." And he is, several times.

Thursdays at St. Mary's are holidays, just as they had been throughout our course in the Society. But I do believe that Thursdays were appreciated much more at St. Mary's than ever before. For one thing, we had learned by this time that one needs a certain amount of recreation if he is to be as efficient as possible in his studies. And, for another thing, we realized that our four years at St. Mary's would be our last chance to enjoy the companionship of our entire group. After our studies we would be separated, with two or three at most going in the same direction. In fact, usually we'd have to go it alone as far as our own group was concerned.

Since St. Mary's is out in the country, there was no problem at all about where we should go on Thursdays. A couple a miles from St. Mary's, over the hills and through the woods, is Pawnee, the principal villa of the theologians. Here the largest group would gather, with a different crew taking turns doing the cooking each Thursday. Our meals at this villa were good and substantial — in keeping with the rustic surrounding. Heat in the winter was by fireplace and pot belly stoves. The entire place had been built by Jesuit scholastics and priests, just as Charbonierre had been.

Since we were such a large group at St. Mary's, not everyone went to Pawnee every week. Many a small group would simply go out in the woods, build a bonfire, and make with the barbecue. (This was my own favorite form of Thursday recreation.) Besides Pawnee, there were several shacks which would accommodate groups up to fifteen or twenty. These were luxurious places made of Kaw River driftwood, mud, and sometimes even some cement. Their names were perfectly in keeping with their Kaw Valley architecture and their accommodations. There was the Pig Sty, the Rat Hole, Tobacco Road, and Skunk Hollow. This latter shack was honored in our time by two events. A cow fell through the roof of the shack (Skunk Hollow was built into the side of a creek bank) and was not discovered until some weeks later, since she had chosen to fall through during the summer, when we were in Wisconsin. It took some time to remove the evidence of her dead presence. A little later, Father Joe Collins happened to be passing by the shack one Sunday, peeked in a window, and found himself eye to eye with an indignant horse. After a few moments of mutual scrutiny, Father Collins opened the door and released this latest tenant. After that, the fences around Skunk Hollow were reinforced.

But to return to the more serious purpose of St. Mary's.

In a sense, the entire course of study is pointed toward our ordination to the priesthood. As Jesuits we have the privilege of being ordained after our third year of theology instead of after our fourth year. So our life for the first three years of theology is filled with anticipation of the priesthood we have been working toward for so long. Indeed, it is during theology, I believe, that our thoughts are really centered on ordination for the first time. We have been too busy studying and working and performing the tasks of the moment up to now.

During our first three years of theology, we serve Mass every day realizing as we do so that in a short time we ourselves will be offering the Holy Sacrifice. We think of the sacraments which we are one day going to confer, especially as we study them in our Rites classes. When our minds are not occupied with necessary studies, our thoughts are usually of the priesthood.

I see no reason here for describing this ceremony of ordination. In the first place you have to see it to be impressed by it. And in the second place it has been explained most adequately in other and better books. Here, I would rather do something that I have tried to do throughout this book, and that is try to state, in some foggy way, just what ordination to the priesthood meant to me. I think I can best do this by citing parts of an article I wrote at the time of my own ordination, trying to get into words what it meant to me to be ordained. It went like this:

I felt in the Sanctuary that day that I was part of a love story. Somehow, I had been raised up until my eyes were on a level with a dividing line of darkness and light.

By casting them down I could see myself struggling and rising and terrified with the thought that the love I sought was where I knew it to be and not in the darkness where I wanted it. By raising my eyes ever so slightly I could see what I had been searching for all along. I could see it and recognize it, but I couldn't describe it. You can't describe a love that waits on a Cross. You can only love it.

There was a mitred figure somewhere in the Sanctuary who called me and imposed his hands on my head and anointed my hands. But the voice that called me seemed to come from the Cross, and somehow it was *His* hands that rested momentarily on my head, then traced the cross in oil on my hands. He made my hands His own hands of love. From now on, they were to give a new divine life in His Name, as I poured the waters of Baptism on foreheads. I was to raise my anointed hand and take away sins in His name. And by some other strange miracle of love I was to hold Him in my hands and give Him to others, somewhat as His spotless Mother held Him in her arms and gave Him to the shepherds to fondle. If love were really blind, I might be able to understand, but this love was omniscient. Only its recipient was blind.

Love held us that day. Somehow, the Blessed Mother and the angels and the whole population of heaven were present. There were others present in the Sanctuary, my companions of many years, who felt as I did, and we loved each other the stronger in Him. There were still others caught up in the same whirlpool of love, kneeling for the blessing He had given me the power to bestow. And there were the absent, that His love made present. A mother, smiling out of eternity, a friend who had hurtled into heaven in a burning plane, others dear to me. They were all there, blessed and touched by my transformed hands.

I might have wondered if there wouldn't come a day when I would fall back to my former groping in the darkness, but I knew that the power which had let me see light and darkness alike would hold me up. I remembered a chalice that had been offered me. A ribbon had bound my hands, a tenuous wispy thing with the strength of God made of the love of God. I had taken the chalice and had let my hands be bound. The Bestower of the chalice and the Binder of my hands would keep His love before me.

You see, it's impossible to write a love story like this. That's why there has only been one undying love story ever written, for only God could squeeze every last drop of blood from His own human Heart.*

I find today, more than six years later, that these words give a somewhat romantic impression, perhaps, of ordination. But that is what it means more than anything else, a love story. Because the priest, besides being the chosen subject of God's love, is also the intermediary between the love of God and man. His is the duty and the privilege of offering God's love to men and of trying somehow to make men see what a tremendous thing is this love that God has for them. And it is his duty also to offer man's love back to God. He stands in the middle, between man and God, and offers the love each one has for the other.

No one else will realize the feeling the priest has as he sits in the dark confessional waiting with great trepidation for his first penitent to come in. No one will know the tremendous respect he will have for the humility and goodness of each of his penitents. Not even he himself can understand the admiration he will have for those with the courage and humility and especially the faith to confess their sins and be absolved. No one can understand or realize how the priest will forget, without even

* From "A Love Story," *Cor*, June, 1949.

*. . . somehow it was His hands that rested momentarily
on my head . . .*

trying, the specific sins he has been told in the confessional. No one, in short, can realize the grace God hands out to those with some courage and confidence in Him.

Again, only the priest will know what it is to approach his first baptism, to wonder if the baby is going to yell so loud that he won't be able to say the words. No one but the priest can know what it is to have two baby eyes watching his every move, or perhaps closed fast in sleep, the picture of peace, or maybe pressed shut while the mouth is wide open yelling to the world that it is receiving the Holy Ghost and renouncing Satan. Only the priest can realize what it means to begin to anoint the head of an infant only to have a pair of baby hands clutch on to his as he approaches its forehead.

Only the priest can know what it means to witness the pledge two people make to each other in the presence of God to live together as man and wife forever. A judge can perform a legal ceremony, but he can hardly call God down to witness, in solemn fashion, the sealing of such a lifelong promise.

Who but a priest could know what it means to stand alone at the altar holding a piece of bread, knowing the tremendous power he will exercise in a moment?

Yes, it is impossible for anyone but a priest to know what ordination can mean. And it is also impossible for him to realize it perfectly.

The emphasis in Tertianship is on the love of God.

IX

AFTER his four years of theology, the Jesuit has one year of training left, his Tertianship. "Tertianship" is a word which has, of course, something to do with a *third* something-or-other. And it is a most appropriate word because the Tertianship is really a third year of Novitiate. Fortunately or unfortunately, or neither one, it lasts not a full year but ten months.

During the year of Tertianship, the Jesuit studies and prays about the interior life, both at his desk and in the chapel. He seeks to ground himself thoroughly in the spiritual life, not only for his own profit and perseverance but so that he can be a safe and sure guide of others. During this year, he again goes through the exercises of the long thirty-day retreat. He finds that the main difference between this long retreat and the first one he made is that, since he had made about fifty retreats in between, there will be nothing exactly new to him. He must therefore pray more about familiar basic truths presented during the retreat, and seek an even deeper knowledge and realization of them.

Up to now, perhaps without really realizing it, his

life has been guided and motivated largely by a sense of duty, obligation, and sacrifice. And while these are all very wonderful motives, now his motive will become not so much that of duty or obligation or even primarily of sacrifice, but more that of love. The Tertianship is, in fact, very often called the school of love. I think that during this year the Jesuit is given a much stronger impetus than ever before to serve God more positively, to work for Him less out of a sense of duty than because he loves Him above all things. It is here that one realizes, perhaps for the first time with perfect clarity, how he can actually love all of God's creatures, mankind first of all, and still love God above all else, but not to the exclusion of all else. The tertian realizes that he is imitating God when he loves the creatures of God, but he realizes, too, that the goodness he sees and loves in creatures is but a shadow of the goodness he loves in God. It is for this reason that he can love God more than creatures and that he is willing, by faith, to save that exclusive sort of love, with which God endows all men, for God Himself in heaven.*

Besides learning as much as possible of the spiritual life in Tertianship, the Jesuit studies his own Institute, the Constitutions of his own order. He studies again the

---

* I would not like to give the impression that this is all new to the tertian. Actually, he is learning none of it for the first time. But very often, things we have known for a long time, even for years, can suddenly become much more clear to us. There can be greater realization of things we have believed all our lives. There can be a deeper understanding of truths we have always known.

spirit of his Society, and learns more fully what is expected of him as a member.

The Jesuit finds, or learns once again, in his Tertianship that there is such a thing as a faulty, superficial spirituality and such a thing as a very solid spirituality. And he finds, too, that the latter is characterized, not by grimness nor by a spirit of edification at any cost, but by something deeper and more hidden. Our Lord told those who heard Him to anoint their heads when they fasted, by which He meant they should not go about clutching their relatively empty stomachs as though the pangs of hunger were driving them mad. The Jesuit in his Tertianship learns that this true spirituality is of a kind which is so much a part of him that it cannot help manifesting itself on the exterior, but which is so deep within him that it manifests itself only spontaneously and not for the sake of edification alone or pride. His spirituality is a *personal* thing, beginning within him and not in externals. In other words, he kneels at prayer in order to adore God. He does not adore God in order to kneel at prayer. The Jesuit learns early in his course, and has it pounded in during Tertianship, that there is no such thing as edification for its own sake. Edification should be an automatic thing, springing naturally from his actions, which in turn have sprung from the love of God. If a religious acts because of the love of God, his actions will automatically be as edifying as they should be.

Again, I think that the tertian Jesuit learns a tremendous lesson in humility. Like all the lessons of Tertianship, this one has been learned before, but it is merely clarified, pounded in, and re-emphasized here. He learns that humility is not calling oneself names or looking down upon oneself but is rather knowing the truth about oneself and acting accordingly. It is acknowledging the gifts God has given him and admitting that they are gifts. I was especially impressed by the humility and edification of a prominent and extremely capable Jesuit friend, Father Dan Lord, when he wrote and produced a very successful play in one of our large cities. He was, during this presentation, getting two or three hours of sleep a night at most. He was constantly backstage in an old sweat shirt, working and directing, driving at every moment. Finally, after the last performance of the play, the audience was on its feet, clamoring for the author and producer to make an appearance. Finally, he did come out on the stage, where he was applauded and applauded until the crowd was tired. Then he bowed, thanked them, and went back to work backstage. A Jesuit scholastic asked him how it felt to receive all that applause. He answered, without thinking, with no intention of trying to edify anybody at all, but simply as always, "It feels pretty good. You see I offer it all up to Christ on the cross, to make up for the fact that He didn't get any of the applause He deserved there." This is great and deep spirituality and humility, something that manifests itself spontaneously because it is part of a man's life.

The only formality which remains for the Jesuit after his Tertianship is the pronouncing of his final vows, which will take place a year or so after his Tertianship. He will then be a completely formed Jesuit.

Tertianship lasts ten months to the day. The prospective tertian keeps busy right up to the moment the doors are opened to admit him. I believe the deadline for tertians to arrive was 6 in the evening in our day. And I think the first one arrived at approximately five minutes to 6. They are not to leave the Tertianship before June 1 of the coming year. The first one out in our time was gone by 5 a.m. of that day. This was not due to any anxiety or hurry to leave the Tertianship, but it was due more to the zeal animating a man who has studied something for fifteen years and is now eager to put it into practice. You can hardly blame him for that. He is quite surprised to find himself still alive after so long a course and now he wants to make use of what he has learned throughout the years before he drops dead.

The Jesuit is in no particular hurry to leave Tertianship.

Smoothness and gentleness must characterize his preaching.

X

THE finished Jesuit leaves Tertianship anxious to share the many things he has learned in the past fifteen years. He wishes to impart to others the truths in his mind and heart and to convince them that there is no happiness except in serving God.

But he doesn't rush out and dash off in all directions. He is assigned to a very definite place where he is given a very definite job to do. Sometimes this job is right in line with his peculiar talents and interests. Very often it is not. The important thing is that he is able and willing to do any job assigned him, so that the Society can function efficiently as a body for the advancement of the kingdom of God.

There is a wide range of occupations for a superior to choose from in placing a subject. Jesuit ministries are many and varied, too many and too varied, perhaps, for the number of men we have. It may seem that we have great numbers, but when they are all distributed to so many jobs, our numbers begin to look extremely skimpy.

At the beginning of 1952, there were 31,561 Jesuits in the world. Of these, 15,593 were priests, while 10,454 were scholastics studying to be priests. There were 5514 brothers. In the eight Jesuit provinces of the United States, there were at the same time 7348 Jesuits of whom 3880 were priests, 2853 were scholastics, and 615 were brothers. In the Missouri Province of the Society, of which I am a member, there were 1162 Jesuits. This number consisted of 635 priests, 403 scholastics, and 124 brothers.

And now, having disposed of the statistics, let's try to find out what happens to the Jesuit after his Tertianship. Is he finished in the sense that he will not do any more work or merely in the sense that he is now a formed Jesuit? As one of our older priests once remarked on the occasion of a young Jesuit's final vows, "There's a young man with a great future behind him."

In the first place, it must be remembered that Jesuits are not Trappist monks. Ours is not a life of contemplation only, but is a mixture of the interior life and a life of active zeal for our neighbor. Much has been written upon which is the highest possible life, the active life, the contemplative life, or a mixture of the two. I do not know enough to enter into a learned discussion on which of these might be the highest life. Nor do I care which is the highest life in itself. For me and for any Jesuit the "highest" life is the one to which we have been called. This is our life and there is no better life for us.

Since we are, then, active as well as contemplative, we are necessarily engaged in a great number of exterior missions. From her very earliest days, the Society of Jesus has considered missionary work her peculiar brand of signal service to the Church. Her sons work their way to the remote corners of the globe, bearing Christ's name to those who have never heard of Him before. The *Epitome of the Institute of the Society of Jesus* puts it thus: "The missions comprise one of the most important works of the Society. All, therefore, should be ready and willing to go on the missions, be prepared to set out for new and strange lands and to spend their lives in any part of the world where there is hope of the greater glory of God and the good of souls."

It is not surprising, then, to find Jesuits all over the world. What is surprising is that occasionally someone (even in print) will consider us as only a teaching order, not realizing the numbers of Jesuits there are on the missions. The latest figures I could gather tell us that there are 5281 Jesuits on the missions, of which 3065 are priests, 1450 are scholastics, and 766 are brothers. Our men are engaged in both foreign missions and home missions for the Indian and the Negro, and, in the southern part of the United States, for everybody.

The Missouri Province* of the Society has as its chief foreign mission Spanish Honduras and British Honduras. This province has also home missions in South Dakota, Wyoming, Omaha, St. Louis, and Trinidad, Colorado. We also have a few men in the Caroline and Marshall Islands, in China, and on the Patna Indian Mission, mis-

---

* In 1954 the Missouri Province was bisected. In this and future references to the province, the old division, including the now Wisconsin Province, will be understood. At present the Wisconsin Province is beginning foreign mission work in Korea.

He is usually stationed very close to home.

sions which are staffed largely by other provinces. It must be remembered that these are the foreign climes haunted by the Missouri Province Jesuits. The Society as a whole is represented in many, many more places and in greater numbers.

Foreign mission work is, of course, glorious work. As I may have mentioned, the happiest years of my life were spent on a foreign mission. The wall of my room was half eaten away by termites. The floor, part wood, part cement, and part brick, was a sort of highway for cockroaches and centipedes and their many friends. One could never sleep unless inside a mosquito net. And yet, as I say, this was the happiest time of my life. The reason is to be found somewhere in the early chapters of this book.

Our work on the missions would, of course, be impossible except for those Jesuits behind the scenes in this country who go about soliciting funds to support the missionaries and for the generous people who welcome them. I think one of the most outstanding examples of generosity I have heard of took place out in Kansas. One of our priests was out preaching about the missions and stopped in at a certain parish. The pastor of this parish had had an uncle who was, I believe, a bishop. The priest had two chalices, one a rather ancient beat-up one, and the other a very nice one that had once belonged to his relative, the bishop. "I did not have any money to give him for the missions," the priest later told me, "so I gave him my chalice." Nor was it the poorer one of the two.

One of the greatest ministries of the Society, sharing honors, in fact, with our ministries in the foreign mission field, is the apostolate of teaching. The *Epitome* states that "The instruction of youth in learning and morals, undertaken out of charity, should be made much of by ours insofar as it is one of the most important ministries

of our Society. The single Provinces should try to set
aside not a few excellent men who will be able to care
for externs with great distinction and profit, by their
teaching, preaching and writing."

Most prominent, of course, among our institutions of
learning are the professional schools, universities and colleges. I should like to mention a few Jesuit universities
and colleges here, with which, perhaps, the reader will
be familiar. There is Regis College, Denver, in colorful,
gorgeous, invigorating Colorado. Other universities and
colleges of the Missouri Province are Creighton University in Omaha, Marquette University in Milwaukee, St.
Louis University, and Rockhurst College in Kansas City,
Missouri.

Some Jesuit universities throughout the country are
quite prominent in various respects. You occasionally see
in the papers mention of a Loyola in Los Angeles, Chicago, Baltimore, or New Orleans. Other Jesuit universities of some note are the University of San Francisco,
Santa Clara University, Xavier of Cincinnati, John Carroll
University of Cleveland, the University of Detroit,
Georgetown in Washington, St. Joseph's College in Philadelphia, the University of Scranton, Canisius College in
Buffalo, Fordham in New York, Boston College, Holy
Cross at Worcester, the University of Seattle, and Gon-
zaga at Spokane.

Usually there will be prep schools connected with or
at least bearing the same name as these colleges and
universities. In the Missouri Province, besides the high
schools bearing the same names as our colleges, there
is Campion High School in Prairie du Chien, Wis-

consin, which has no college connected with it. Teaching in high school and teaching in college are two quite different things, each of them pleasant in its own way, each having its peculiar headaches. Ordinarily the Jesuit high school teacher has his time more taken up with extracurricular activities than does the college teacher. He will find himself in charge of publications or of a speech group, directing sodalities and athletics, counseling and guiding the students. Naturally, all of these activities are also indulged in by the college teacher, but I do believe that they must be given more time and attention by the high school teacher, largely because of the lower stage of maturity and dependability of high school students.

Another sort of teaching takes place in parishes, where the Jesuit will find himself teaching religion to the children. One of our priests told me the first time he walked into a third grade classroom to teach catechism to the youngsters, he was taken aback by the small size of the members of his audience. And his first question was not to the children at all but to the teacher: "What language do you use when they're this little?"

Another ministry which Jesuits are actively engaged in is parish work. Usually, you will find the Jesuit parish connected with their college or university. But besides these parishes there are others also, independent of any school.

The Jesuits also help very often in parishes which are not their own. Each week end, you will find a great percentage of the Jesuit priests of the community going out to help in parishes around the city. The bigger feast days, such as Christmas and Easter, are perfect duds in

Jesuit houses until later on in the evening, because either all the priests are still out working in parishes around the city or they are resting up from having been out working in these parishes.

We also go to say Mass and to hear confessions at convents whenever called upon and whenever we have enough men to do so. We call this sort of parish work "supply."

We begin our supply work with our lives as priests. At St. Mary's, during our fourth year of theology, we were allowed to go out and help in the various parishes in Kansas. I must say that, for the most part, we are always treated royally by the pastors and assistants at these parishes and it is a great experience to know men such as they. Without detracting in any way from the other men I have met on supply jobs, I should like to say here that the greatest of them all in my mind is Father Harry Cunningham, a pastor in a seemingly insignificant little town in Kansas. The world in its ignorance will probably never realize Father Cunningham's stature. I know this, that after my final exam in theology I went up to his parish for about a week to share in his peace. And I was not disappointed.*

And then, on the other side of the glass, is the exception to the general rule: the priest who treats us well enough, perhaps, but a little waspishly. To date, I

* I realize that I should give some explanation of just why I think so much of Father Cunningham, but I refrain from doing so to avoid embarrassing him. Let it be enough to say that Christ must think a lot of him, too, otherwise He wouldn't have blessed him with the special gift of suffering and the grace to use it properly.

have encountered only one such priest. I visited him for Holy Week one year. He was nervous and, as a result, tended to be a little critical and to shout a bit. He had heard somewhere that it was the custom to have ham for Easter and besides he seemed to be trying to get rid of the ham he had on hand, by serving it at every meal at which meat was allowed for the entire week. Another one of our men who had helped him out was asked not to cross his legs while sitting in his chair because it was "hard on the furniture." When all our work of Holy Week was finished, this paragon of hospitality drove me home from his parish, with his police dog, of which he was very fond, in the back of the car. When we got to St. Mary's, we stopped at a gas station and Father, too nervous to remain in the car, got out to pace up and down while the attendant filled the tank. When we stopped, the dog was lying on the floor in the back of the car, out of sight. I was sitting in front next to the driver's seat. After the attendant finished filling the tank, he took his chamois and wiped the windshield.

Then, as he began on the side windows, the pastor shouted at him: "Don't bother with those. That damn fool in there will slobber all over them anyhow!"

The attendant looked carefully into the car, his eyes bulging. The only "damn fool" he could see in the car was another priest — myself — at the moment occupied in trying to slide down a little lower in the front seat and snapping my fingers so the man could see that the dog in the back was being referred to as the slobberer. The dog, however, was cunning enough to remain hidden. I considered the situation extremely funny, but my friend the pastor didn't seem to see anything humorous in it at all.

Come to think of it, maybe he hadn't referred to the dog after all.

Another ministry of the Society is that of preaching. Of course, all Jesuits do some preaching, especially in their supply work. But certain ones are assigned to what we call a "Mission Band" as their permanent job. These men go about, living out of a suitcase for most of their lives, preaching missions and retreats in any city to which they are called. They have a hard life, always traveling as they do and never putting down roots, but it is a life of great zeal and good work.

We also run a number of retreat houses for men. Retreats — or days of recollection — are given for groups of men in these houses, mostly on week ends. The men will come, say, on a Thursday night and remain at the place through Friday, Saturday, and Sunday, making a three-day retreat during this time, considering prayerfully their relation to God and the progress they are making toward heaven. Again, this is a very important work of the Society.

Another large order the Society has to fill is the spreading and seeing to the smooth functioning of the sodality movement, an organization whose members strive to *practice* Christian perfection in a better-than-ordinary way. This organization has its central headquarters in St. Louis at *The Queen's Work* building. Instrumental, of course, in organizing and pushing the sodality in America, and recognized as such by the Holy Father, was Father

Dan Lord. And we cannot mention his name without recalling the tremendous work he did, not only in the sodality, but in many other fields. He produced numerous plays and pageants, which have been recognized, by authorities on these things, as excellent productions. Everyone knows, too, the vast number of pamphlets he wrote, the sale of which has totaled over seventeen million copies. At the time of his death he was engaged, not only in writing more than any ten men could write, but in promoting an organization known as the "Knights and Handmaids of the Blessed Sacrament," a beautiful idea for the promotion of devotion to the Blessed Sacrament.

The Society has workers, too, on many publications in America. Besides publishing pamphlets, she staffs *America*, the *Theological Digest, Thought, The Messenger of the Sacred Heart, Jesuit Missions*, and other publications.

She is engaged, too, in social work and in labor relations groups. There are Jesuit experts in these fields and there are Jesuits who have helped to settle strikes and labor difficulties in many places. Rev. John Corridan, S.J., for instance, has received national recognition for his fearless work in helping to clean up the New York water-front situation. Father Dennis J. Comey, S.J., well known as an arbitrator of water-front disputes in Philadelphia, was appointed by President Eisenhower to a three-member fact-finding board to mediate the East Coast dock dispute. Father Leo Brown, S.J., of St. Louis was also given a presidential appointment as a member of the panel to settle labor disputes in government atomic-energy projects. Previously, Father Brown had been distinguished by the *St. Louis Labor Journal* as "Labor's Man of the Year," with this citation: "He was the only man trusted by both sides in the showdown [of the St. Louis Teamsters' strike]. Many other times during the year his sage advice has saved many other unions from heading into trouble."

During the war, a number of Jesuits were chaplains in the various armed forces, and many, among them Congressional Medal of Honor winner Father Joseph T. O'Callaghan, S.J., of *U.S.S. Franklin* fame, were decorated for valor. They were taken away from their other work for this all-important duty of serving our country and serving those who served our country.

The Sacred Heart radio program, originating from St. Louis, and the League of the Sacred Heart are organized and promoted by Jesuits. The last I heard, there were more than nine hundred stations broadcasting the daily Sacred Heart Program.

A certain number of Jesuits each year have to be channeled into special studies, so that the Society can have an adequate number of experts in every field. Each year a number of men will be sent to different universities for further study in such subjects as science, speech, education, English, library science, and especially theology and philosophy. From my point of view, this is a life which really demands much self-sacrifice. Of course, I am prejudiced in this belief since study has usually seemed to me a necessary evil rather than a pleasure. And I could hardly visualize myself enduring any more of this necessary evil, after spending fifteen years of study in the

Society. But I am sure that among our special students are those with enough love for study to find it pleasurable, at times.

Besides the ministries which we exercise toward the people around us, there are some very important ministries which the Jesuit must exercise toward his own men. Our own priests, scholastics, and brothers make an eight-day retreat every year. And the younger men of the Society add two three-day retreats to this. Someone has to give all these retreats. So there are Jesuits who give a goodly number of retreats to their own men. Since we have made so many retreats, it takes an excellent retreat master to interest and inspire our own men. It is not strange, then, that we notice traits in some retreat masters which, I am sure, others would not be aware of. There was the retreat master, for instance, who, when giving points for a meditation on death put on such a ghoulish smile that he almost scared us all to death. And there was the very holy and very delightful one who, when speaking to us of indifference to creatures, said, with admirable simplicity, "We do not choose our own food. If we did, perhaps we could digest it."

One of the most memorable three-day retreats during my course in the Society took place at St. Mary's. The retreat master was a pastor, used to the larger surroundings of his parish. (I understand that he cost us fifty-seven dollars for a single evening.) At Benediction, he burned the rug with incense because of a little too much enthusiasm in swinging the censer, broke the tabernacle key and a couple of other small items. In a larger sanctuary, he wouldn't have damaged anything, I'm sure, but the smaller surroundings of St. Mary's did seem like a china shop with him in action. It was little peculiarities such as these which helped to make retreats interesting and memorable as well as profitable.

A very great and very difficult and very thankless apostolate which some Jesuits are engaged in is that of teaching our own men. I am sure that there is some gratitude expressed in our early days in the Society toward our teachers, but as we grow older and study longer we do not tend to be too grateful to those who teach us, at least we do not express our gratitude often. It is a wonderful thing to teach boys in school, but I imagine it is very difficult to teach our own men. The Jesuit wants to exercise his zeal, but how can he exercise it on those who have had his identical training? I know that underneath all our lack of expression of thanks, however, there is tremendous gratitude in our hearts for all our teachers, for those who guided us and taught us during our lengthy course of studies. In case there is any doubt left in the minds of those who have taught this particular Jesuit, let me say now that, though I sat in class like a dynamic block of wood, I do appreciate the effort they expended trying to make me a learned Jesuit. It wasn't their fault if they didn't succeed perfectly.

The exercise of thoughtfulness and kindness is not usually referred to as an apostolate. But it seems to me that it is, in a sense, a very genuine apostolate. The kindly charity which Jesuits manifest, not only toward externs but particularly toward one another, is a very great implicit apostolate. I once spent a year as a patient in a hospital. Naturally, I missed my fellow Jesuits most. But whenever they could, they came in groups or alone to see me, although the hospital was more than seventy miles from their home and they were very busy. Many who hardly knew me dropped in as frequently as they could. I was particularly impressed when one Eastern Jesuit, Father Ed Rooney, Prefect General of Studies for the American Assistancy of the Society, came to see me, although he didn't know me from Adam. He had simply heard that there was a Jesuit in the hospital and had come to see him.

It is no idle remark that St. Ignatius makes when he speaks in his rule of "the interior law of charity and love" as the guiding force in the Jesuit's life. And, though the Jesuit may perhaps seem like an offhand and even cynical person today, he is, in reality, completely sold on St. Ignatius and his rules, and ready to practice the charity of Christ on every occasion and in every possible way.

In speaking of apostolates, there is another that must not be left out — the apostolate of sickness and suffering. I am certain that some sick Jesuits do as much for the Kingdom of God by offering up their prayers and sufferings as they can possibly do by any mere external activity. We are especially convinced of this fact here at Regis College because of one member of our community, Father Al Gage, who has been hospitalized now since 1948. Any single one of our community can tell you with perfect truth that our most valuable Jesuit in these parts is Father Gage.

There is another form of apostolate of the Society which I can best introduce by quoting Father James

Brodrick, S.J. In one of his many interesting books, Father Brodrick mentions a superior whose relationship toward his community was governed by the motto, "We have a rule and according to that rule he must die." I have never, fortunately, in my years in the Society, met a superior who fulfilled this description exactly. Most of them have been very understanding, very good friends as well as good superiors. Some have, of course, fitted this favorable description better than others.

To be a superior in the Society of Jesus is as much an apostolate as any of our external ministries. In many ways, it is much more difficult, I am sure, than working with externs. For one thing, no one is a hero to his own community. And a Jesuit who is filled with zeal wants to exercise that zeal on the other people around him and not on his own community. He feels that his fellow Jesuits will get along quite well by themselves without the help of his particular brand and degree of zeal. So when a man is assigned to one of our houses as a superior, he is occupied in a work of zeal which requires blind faith to perceive.*

There is really little basis of comparison between army brass and superiors in the Society of Jesus. Ours is a much more personal government, and therefore much more elastic and relaxed than the army system of officers and men. The Society is governed, in the first place, by a Father General, who resides at Rome and who normally

---

* Such an attitude, of course, comes from a natural viewpoint. Supernaturally speaking, our zeal is best exercised through obedience, and a superior knows this if anyone does. However, he is still human enough to want to have his cake and eat it too.

holds office for life. Under him are several assistants from different countries who serve the General in at least an advisory capacity. Each country is divided into provinces, and over each province is a Father Provincial. Over each house is a Father Rector, and, helping him in the government of that house, taking care especially of temporal affairs, is a Father Minister. There are also various minor officials.

Since most of one's orders come from his immediate local superiors, and since he very often knows these superiors quite well even before they take office, there is a great spirit of camaraderie, combined with respect, between superiors and subjects.

During the period of my teaching days in Belize, Father Joseph Zuercher, then provincial of the Missouri Province, came to visit us one year. Now it so happened that, at that particular time, I was teaching Virgil in my third- and fourth-year Latin classes, and the section we were studying was about Laocoön and his sons who had a great deal of trouble with a couple of huge snakes. In keeping with the text, the boys one day brought me a very apt gift, a snake — although a rather small one. After class, I took it up to my room and, seeing no place to keep it at the moment, put it in the bottom drawer of my desk. When I returned to my room after study hall about 9 o'clock that night and opened the drawer, I found that the snake had decided not to wait. So I promptly went from room to room inquiring if anyone had seen my snake. I got some rather queer looks from those I questioned, but none so queer as that which I received from Father Zuercher.

"Have you seen my snake?"

"Have you seen my snake anywhere?" I asked him.
"Snake?"

"Yes, I had him in the desk drawer and he seems to
have escaped somewhere."

"Where do you live?"

I pointed straight up. "Right above you," I told him.

Father Zuercher, dignified provincial that he was, was
not too dignified to see the humor in it. But I never did
find that snake.

For a time, while we were philosophers at St. Louis,
our superior was Father Eugene Murphy, now director
of the Sacred Heart Program. We were young men
with exuberant spirits, as the saying goes, and he

understood that fact perfectly. Fresh from Florissant, we were surprised to notice that, when Father Murphy would make an especially fine point during an instruction, the philosophers would applaud him. It was a new type of spiritual instruction for us. Then there was the Mothers' Day when we placed a huge bouquet of flowers outside his door in honor of the occasion. Most of us feel sure that we are better religious for having been exposed to the unstrained spiritual atmosphere which Father Murphy could engender with his easy personality and the consequent trust he put in us.

Occasionally, the superiors at St. Mary's and some of our foreign theologians had a difficult time understanding each other. On one occasion, one of our superiors suffered a severe shock when he reprimanded one of the foreign scholastics for breaking silence. The scholastic's English could not even be dignified by calling it "broken." At any rate, he became quite incensed with the superior because of the mild, but probably well-deserved reprimand. He figured that he was being treated more like a schoolboy than like a man, though his opinion was definitely open to question. He tried to tell the superior that he was in his thirties and would have been a big man in the world by this time. What he actually said was something quite different. Looking the superior straight in the eye, he said, "I am a man. In the world I have five children." The superior, taking him literally at first, was quite jolted, until he realized that "I have" should have been "I would have by this time."

There were, too, embarrassing moments occasionally with superiors, made more embarrassing and consequently more humorous because of the smallness and lack of seriousness of the situations. Father Murphy, who tended to simplify things a great deal, got the idea when we were philosophers that when anyone was speaking especially loud it was a certain scholastic, whom we shall call Mr. Jones. One day when he heard loud talking on the first floor, he leaned over the third floor banister and shouted down: "Quiet, Mr. Jones!" And a voice right next to his ear asked innocently, "Did you want me, Father?" Father Murphy looked sheepishly around into the face of the real Mr. Jones.

Then there was the time Father Dick Pates was standing by our bulletin board at St. Mary's during a period of silence. He was making a few remarks about something on the bulletin board, while four or five of us stood behind him, also reading the note on the board. As he rambled on he didn't realize that the original audience of four or five had drifted off and was no longer there, until he turned around in the midde of a sentence and looked straight into the eye of Father Herbst, our superior. He was so caught by surprise that all he could do was tip his biretta and walk away, rather quickly, but not before Father Herbst had looked down from about a foot above him and told him to shut up and go to his room. Both of them had a hard time keeping a straight face.

I was once standing looking at the same bulletin board and thinking that my friend Father Joe Sheehan was standing at my right shoulder just behind me. As I was leaving the board, I dug my elbow quite effectively into his stomach. The stomach seemed considerably softer than Father Sheehan's, however. It belonged to the Spiritual Father of the theologians, not a superior, but a man of far too much dignity to have his stomach invaded by an elbow.

I remember the time also that two scholastics, newly arrived from Florissant, were serving the Mass of Father Joe Horst, our superior of the Philosophate in St. Louis. When Father came down to say the prayers at the end of Mass, both scholastics forgot to push over a pad for him to kneel on. Finally, at the last moment, one of them thought of it and pushed over the pad just as Father Horst knelt down. The result of this delicate timing was that Father Horst, all unknowing, said the prayers while kneeling not only on a rubber kneeling pad but on a scholastic's hand.*

Just as we had all kinds of companions in our course of study and later on, so we had all kinds of superiors: tall ones, short ones, friendly ones, and those who were rather reserved. Naturally, there were those we could talk to freely and those who were a bit remote. I do not

---

* Father Horst was undoubtedly one of the most lovable superiors we have had. We were fond of him for many reasons, chiefly, perhaps, because we sensed his concern for us and his devotion to our interests. His Germanisms in class, such as "You're beating the bush around" made his lectures memorable as well as orderly and precise. Most memorable of all, though, was the instruction he gave us before our departure for villa each summer. "For those who have a hang-over in Chicago," he would say when he meant "a stopover in Chicago." "As for the swimming suits," he would tell us, "they should be worn. You can get brown — but not all over." Then he would smile indulgently at our laughter. As we might have expected, Father Horst died, with no preceding sickness, shortly after being transferred from the Philosophate in St. Louis.

wish to speak about any particular superiors here except to mention two. The first was really not a superior at all at the time (though he is now), but he did hold the position of *Socius* (companion or assistant) to the Provincial for about seventeen years. And in that job he did an inestimable amount of good for us scholastics. Jesuits of our province will know that I am speaking of Father William Fitzgerald who was always a great friend to all of us, even though his job forced him to move in very superior circles. Only God knows how many young men in the Society he encouraged to keep going when the going was a little rough and only God will know the kindness Father Fitz showed and still shows toward so many of his Jesuit brothers.

The other person was one of the best superiors I have ever been privileged to be under. He was completely fair, never cold or remote, but always willing to listen, always anxious to hear both sides of a question. This was Father David Hickey, my superior in Belize and who is now Bishop Hickey in the same place. To me, he comes close to fulfilling the ideal that St. Ignatius had in mind when he endorsed the system of superior-subject for his Society.

Yes, the Jesuits have many ministries in which to employ themselves. By certain standards, they study for a long, long time, but every bit of what they learn is to be used later in one way or another. And the one guide as to how they will use their knowledge and experience is contained in the motto, *Ad Majorem Dei Gloriam,* "All for the greater glory of God."

Calmly, unhurriedly, and efficiently, he goes about
his daily duties.

EPILOGUE

$\mathbf{S}$INCE a large part of this book consists of reminiscences, I know no better way of bringing it to a close than by further reminiscences, by going back on a visit to the place where my Jesuit training began, St. Stanislaus Seminary at Florissant, Missouri.

For some years after we left Florissant, a rather religious sneer went with the expression "The House of Bread," in reference to the Novitiate. We thought that we were well out of the place. And we thought, too, though we had been warned about this very thing, that we were a little above some of the practices of our Alma Mater. Not that we felt that any of the religious ideas or duties that we had learned there were ridiculous or out of place. By no means. But we did feel that we were more mature (which was true in a sense), and that now we were formed spiritual men (which was far from true). And we looked back on the days at St. Stanislaus with the condescension that a sixteen-year-old adolescent has for a fourteen-year-old boy.

But it didn't take us long to realize, if not to admit,

that St. Stanislaus was really the House of Bread, the sort of bread we prayed for every day in the *Our Father,* "Give us this day our daily bread." We began to see that the things we had learned there were lasting things. We began to wish for the faithfulness of those days, for the good will that drove us through three or four years there. It wasn't long, either, before we found a new intention in our prayers, almost automatically, the fervent prayer that the novices and juniors being trained at Florissant would absorb every bit of their training so that the effect would be permanent and lasting and so that the Society could raise up great instruments in the hands of God.

When I last visited St. Stanislaus Seminary at Florissant (February 25 to March 6, 1953), it had been almost seventeen years since I had first come there and a long, long time since I had seen the place. I was a bit apprehensive as to what I would find. All of us know, you see, that in these days of greater minds, the Society, too, is following the trend by filling her ranks with the upper strata of intellects. So I fully expected, on arriving at the seminary for my retreat, to see a generation of novices and juniors endowed with outsize heads and high sloping intellectual foreheads. It was very cheering and encouraging to see only one high forehead among all the novices and juniors. And that one wasn't sloping at all. It was just so high it went back almost to the neckbone. I felt better, too, when the reader in the refectory one day mispronounced four or five Latin words in two minutes. It was at that moment that I began to feel at home.

It was a shock and yet a wonderful thing to look around

and see the apple-cheeked young novices and juniors. A shock, because it was then I realized how long it had been since we had been in their places. And I wondered if we had ever looked that young.*

It was a thrill to see the novices, with their rosaries in their cinctures, and the juniors, distinguished by their birettas or by the fact they could walk two and two at recreation. You could still spot a novice in the chapel from a great distance. For who else but a novice or a contortionist could work himself into such prayerful positions?

I was happy to see, too, that the haircuts of the novices and juniors were just as bad as ever, and looked more like the random nibblings of a hungry rat than anything else. This made me happy, because I recalled that from the day Father Jim Hanley and I had been appointed as barbers, neither of us had ever turned out a good haircut, especially on each other. In fact, our greatest argument came from trying to decide who would cut whom last when it came our turn for a haircut.** I recalled, too, Father Hanley's habit of throwing chunks

---

* Later, when I looked at our novice picture in an old album, I saw that we had not only looked that young, but I, for one, had also looked completely callow and stupid. I could possibly have been mistaken for one of the calves on the farm, except I did usually walk only on my hind legs.

** There is some truth to the saying in the Society, "Once a barber, always a barber." Both Father Hanley and I kept nibbling away right up to ordination. However, in one's last year as a barber at St. Mary's, he is accorded a rare privilege. He is allowed to choose his customers instead of having them choose or refuse him. It was for this reason that I cut very little hair in my final year in the profession,

of steel wool or old rope down in front of his victim's eyes as he made the sound effects with the scissors.

I could not help thinking, too, of the difference in our ideals in those days and now. Then, ideals had been vague things, with great generous resolutions involved, but without the particular directions that they later assumed. Our ideals now were probably greater and stronger and more precise. But we had not foreseen, as novices, the sometimes terrific struggle it would be keeping them. And it's just as well we did not see it. Because we would probably not have seen the overwhelming grace that would be helping us to win the struggle, helping us "to give and not to count the cost, to fight and not to heed the wounds." We might not have realized that we were anticipating tomorrow's trials with today's graces.

Whenever you revisit an old familiar place, you naturally look around to see if any of your old friends are still there. And as I looked around at Florissant, I saw only two of the priests who had been members of the faculty in our day there. These, however, were the two whom we certainly would have voted the most likely to survive, Father Aloysius Jacobsmeyer and Father Francis Preuss. I saw the latter in the garden one day, watching a junior cut a limb off a tree and giving him appropriate directions. He had done a lot of this with us when we were juniors. As I watched him now, I recalled the time that he was directing a junior in cutting off a limb on which the junior's ladder rested.

---

since I beat my fellow barbers out in selecting for customers ten of the most hairless Jesuits at St. Mary's.

Many of the brothers who had been there with us were still around: Brother Du Charme, Brother Recker, Brother Husemann, Brother Joe Siehr, Brother Eufinger, Brother Eilert, Brother Schwendemann, and Brother Daniels — who got his start in the powerhouse, an occupation which trained him remotely for his present job of infirmarian. He and I had more in common than the fact that we both had been novices together. It seems that each of us had once had the same ambition in life, to pilot a one-man streetcar. We have decided, in this modern day, to convert to a bus.

These were the old familiar faces at Florissant. But there were some new ones, contemporaries, or near-contemporaries rather, of mine. There was Father Tom Halley, from my own class; and Father Joe Costello, one of the sharpest minds I have looked in awe upon, who now teaches the juniors. Father Frank Guentner is now the distinguished *Socius* to the Master of Novices. Father Walt Harris at the time of my visit bellered out the grace before and after meals with great resonance. This is not surprising, since we who knew him recall his constant practicing of vowel sounds and such in the subterranean caverns that honey-combed the old Novitiate. And we recall, too, the way his neck muscles bulged while he sang in chapel. One learns to spot the future minister very early in the Society.

The road still winds through St. Joe's Woods to the villa of Charbonierre, on the heights overlooking the river. This road, to me at least, has always, in almost any season, seemed lovely. It is especially so, perhaps, in the fall. But even in bleak February and March I found it pleasing because, perhaps, of the promise that the green buds and shoots of grass already gave.

As one leaves the gate behind the Novitiate, he crosses Howdershell Road, goes past the cow barns, past the seismograph station and a couple of pastures. As I passed the barns, I noticed the present inhabitant of the bull pen. He was an exact replica of the bull who had been there in our day. There was this difference, however: our bull had been sufficiently bull-like to be violent while this one reminded me of a placid Southern gentleman. He lay there with complete indifference even to the cows on the other side of the fence, as though he were far superior to such things. However, the full maternity ward to the north belied his indifference.

On my nostalgic revisit, I walked to the end of one of the pastures, then turned to the right along a fence and descended into a wooded gulley, through which sometimes ran a rather listless creek. It was by this same gulley that I had once seen a comedy acted out. I had wandered up that way during one of our *triduums* and had sat on a bank watching nothing in particular. Suddenly, there had been yipes and frantic barking in the distance. Over the hill and across the gulley from me came the flashing figure of a red fox. No sooner was he out of sight of his pursuers over the rise than he turned sharply to his right dashed along a hedgerow up over the road and disappeared. In a moment, two terriers came yapping over the hill in hot pursuit. The one nearest to me decided to turn right at the proper place, but his companion decided to go straight. The result was a collision, and the fight which ensued between the two clowns ruined their chances of ever finding the fox, who was probably not too far away laughing at them. It is doubtful what they would have done had they caught him anyway.

I remembered all that as I walked through the woods, following the now dry creek bed to another familiar spot, a hollowed-out place with smooth banks and huge trees. It had been beautiful and green one afternoon when another junior and I had taken a walk out there and had sat down to relax and probably collect chiggers. It had been one of these Juniorate afternoons on which we were allowed either to study or to take recreation. As far as I was concerned, there was never any choice. I was just beginning to relax when my companion voiced his wish to go home and study. The two attitudes were perfect keys to our respective personalities.

I passed over what had been our golf course, the aristo-cratic Heifer Heights. Here, Father Bob Lambeck and Father Martin Vaske had pounded golf balls so far that it was a wonder they ever found them.

Along the path at one point was a wayside shrine. On the most beautiful oak tree in St. Joe's Woods, and perhaps in the whole state of Missouri, was a simple cross. Here, too, we had often paused to say a prayer to Christ crucified. It was most fitting that He should be there to remind us from that particular oak.

A little farther on was the old pond where we used to skate. It seemed a good deal smaller now. There was once a rumor that the soap we used in the Novitiate was cut, during certain seasons, from the slime of this pond.

I walked back up to the cinder road once more and followed it down to the pump house. Things were almost exactly the same there, except for the new bridge over the creek. There was the same primitive swinging gate at the top of the steps going down to the pump house. There was the identical shrine of our Lady where we always stopped on our way to Charb. There was the same old inscription before the shrine:

> Oh, Mary! Oh, my Mother,
> Remember that I am thine.
> Preserve me, defend me,
> As thy property and possession.

In the years that had gone by, she certainly had done just that.

Past the pump house, over a few hills, and you come to Charbonierre. Charbonierre itself has changed, perhaps, more than anything around Florissant. As you come over the last hill before arriving at Charb, the first thing you see is the new chapel, which is really a thing of beauty. Farther down the hill, you come upon the dormitory, which was new in our day. Then, going up a slight rise to another hill, you come to the refectory which was built by our group of juniors, mostly by Father Earl Kurth, now superior of St. Stephen's Indian Mission in Wyoming. The day I visited the place I did not have a key, so I contented myself with looking in the windows and noticing, rather smugly, that many of the decorations inside were those perpetrated by my contemporaries.

I walked up from the refectory of Charbonierre to De Smet Mound, the highest spot of the villa, and looked down toward the ball field, along the rugged path we had rocketed along on bobsleds and wondered how we had done it without breaking our necks.

I could not help thinking how history sometimes goes backward when I looked down and noticed that the old outhouse, which had been moved with great fuss and ceremony in our day, was now back in its old spot, where it commanded an excellent view of the road, and vice versa.

I walked down the path, or what was left of it, to the site of our old refectory. It was entirely overgrown with weeds, and the only evidence that there had ever been a building there was a cracked piece of pipe stuck in the ground. Next to the refectory had once been a gazebo, which was represented now by only a lonely piece of tattered tar paper.

Through the weeds I could perceive the stone wall near which Fathers Bob Lakas and Hilary Brozowski had labored so long and hard planting flowers.

The old refectory had stood on the edge of a very high cliff overlooking the river. Now I walked north along the edge of that cliff toward the rock gazebo which commanded a perfect view of the river and where we had spent so many convivial hours. At least the gazebo was still there. When I went inside, a log was still smoldering from yesterday's fire. (The juniors always go to Charb on Thursday. My visit was on Friday.) There was a strong smell of coffee in the little room. The huge old log table was still there, and a few of the ancient songbooks that we had used to such advantage.

From the windows of the gazebo you could look down on the river in one direction, upon a shrine of our Lady in another, and upon the old swimming pool and bathhouse a little above the shrine.

When I had scrambled down the hill to the shrine, I noticed that it looked very much the same, the most notable difference being that Mary was sporting a gorgeous new dress of paint. But the place remained essentially unchanged, as did the rock Stations of the Cross. I was much interested in the log steps which circled up from either side of the shrine, because Father Adrian Kochanski and I had labored so long and with such great diligence on their construction. As I stood before Mary's statue and finished a *Memorare*, I could almost hear the old manuductor* shout out, "Everything everywhere," as he had when we novices visited Charbonierre, which wasn't very often.

The swimming pool looked exactly the same, as did the bathhouse, except that the wooden floor of the latter seemed to echo much more hollowly now as I walked through it alone.

Immediately behind the bathhouse stood the stump monument of the first tree, but by no means the last, that Father Kochanski and I had cut down at Charbonierre. And I could see now, looking at the stump, why, even when we had seemingly cut through the entire tree, it still had stood there and defied us. I remembered the great glee that Father Preuss had made no effort to hide when told of this phenomenon and how ghoulishly he had laughed as he told us to knock it over with wedges.

----

* A "manuductor" is a very dignified novice official. During his hour in the sun, he puts up signs and notices telling the novices what is coming up next or he sneaks up on a novice to tell him that Father Master would like to see him.

Another historical stump stood near the place where the old dam had been. We had surprised a whole family of flying squirrels and a huge red squirrel as that rotten tree had come down and shattered on the dam. I remembered how Father Kurth and I, using heavy sledges, in an effort to tear down the dam, had worn our hands out without making much impression on the thing. Someone of a later generation must have discovered some dynamite.

Down the hill and toward the river from the swimming pool was one of my old hangouts, the *herpetarium*. It had once been a pump house, but Father Walter Ong and Father George Pieper had converted it into a *herpetarium* or snake house. Here they had collected all available species of snake, and I had succeeded them in this noble work. At one time I had been the proud owner of around two hundred snakes, due largely to a ribbon snake's giving birth one fine day to about one hundred and fifty young ribbons. But the glory of the *herpetarium* had faded. Most of the walls were gone and there were only three empty cages left.

A short distance from the snake house was a huge, long slough of the Missouri River, where we had skated in the winter and around which we had often walked and, more or less, explored and collected snakes.

I went back up to the main section of Charbonierre by way of the steep stone steps up which we had so often toted logs for some reason or other, largely, I would say now, just to be toting logs.

On the way home, I passed along a hill where I recall I had almost been the cause of my own death and that of two other Jesuits — a priest and a junior — and two horses. They (the horses) were hitched to a farm wagon. I can still recall the expression or rather the lack of it on the priest's face when, as we were barreling headlong down the hill, he asked me why I didn't put on the brake, and I told him I had never driven these things before and had no idea where the brake, if there was one, might be. The gatepost that we clipped off as we shot through the open gate (fortunately it *was* open) at the foot of the hill was still gone about sixteen years later.

But enough for the environs. What about the seminary itself? The first difference one notices is that when standing anywhere on the grounds of the seminary and looking down into the valley, he sees a valley filled with homes and not the empty rolling land of our day. Civilization has moved much closer to St. Stanislaus. The front lane, which leads from the highway to the seminary, looks exactly the same but much shorter than it did the day Father Eugene Korth and I were walking up its unbelievable length toward home at the end of our record forty-mile walk.

The garden, though it does seem smaller with the new Juniorate infringing upon it, is as lovely as ever. While I was there on my visit, we had one of those wet snows that weighed down the branches of the trees until you wondered why they didn't break. It was a snow, I recalled, such as we had had one Christmas Eve in which I had sloshed around for about an hour trying to get my miserable youthful feelings in order.

I almost got run over several times while walking in the garden, because the novices no longer say their rosary in one group but in two groups, so that while you keep your eye on Group A, Group B will come up behind you and push you off the walk while hurling prayers at you. I was pleased to notice two or three novices sporting rather weird costumes. One was especially outstanding, I thought, with a flat black hat and a sky-blue jacket over his black cassock. All of which made me realize again that novices never change.

The little stone shrine of our Lady still stands in the same place it always did. Inside is one of the loveliest statues of her that I have ever seen. I suppose that an artist would probably consider it as of not much value, but the artist would have never been a novice who had seen her smile down upon his sorrows and joys.

It was to this shrine that we used to dash before Midnight Mass on Christmas, driven on by the apocryphal tradition that the first one there on Christmas Eve would never leave the Society. The tradition had been purposely exploded by a novice one year who had already decided to leave. Besides, the tradition was a dangerous one, as Father Bill McEvoy, who had broken his arm in an effort to get there first, will testify.

It was on the altar of this shrine that we had placed our feeble efforts at writing poetry to the Mother of God during the month of May. It was in this shrine that Father Joe Sheehan (now *Socius* to the Master of Novices at Oshkosh, Wisconsin) and I had constructed a Christmas crib to end all cribs. It was made of wrapping paper, glue, and sand, the entire mess supposedly formed into rocks. The crib *was* a beauty, but there was a serious difficulty: the smell of glue was so overpowering as to ruin even a novice's devotion. The incense we kept burning in order to combat the smell of glue didn't have a chance.

On the wall next to the statue of the Blessed Virgin in the shrine is a plaque that has always interested me. It reads like this:

> In your Charity
> Please pray for
> Mrs. Margaret Barney Blake
> And her dear ones
> Living and dead
> RIP
> July 19, 1935

I have often wondered what sort of man was Barney, a man responsible for such a musical combination of names as Margaret Barney Blake.

I noticed, as I left the shrine, that a fresh vase of flowers stood before our Lady's statue.

In our day, the statue of the Sacred Heart had stood on the highest spot at the border of the seminary grounds, so that He seemed to be holding His hands over us in blessing. For some reason or other, He has now been relegated to a clump of trees off to the side, where He looks more like a cheer leader standing in front of a towering basketball team. But then He really is a cheer leader in a way, I guess. In the place of prominence once occupied by the statue of the Sacred Heart is a statue of the Guardian Angel. Which only goes to show that even guardian angels should have guardian angels. I have felt this way since my first year of Novitiate when I used to whisper a pious prayer to Joe, my own guardian angel, asking him to please keep me awake during spiritual reading. One day, while dozing during spiritual reading, I fell off the chair with a great clatter, arousing not only myself but everyone, it seemed, for miles around, which goes to show further that a guardian angel can get a bit rough.

Down in the old field where we used to have our games and where the novices and juniors still get their exercise, there are a great number of improvements, with the new swimming pool on the side of the road that leads to the field and two wonderful basketball courts. But the tennis courts are just the same and the handball courts are practically the same. The same shrine of the Holy Family stands just above the tennis courts. The same baseball field where we had such wonderful games and rhubarbs which would make Leo Durocher seem like Casper Milquetoast is still there. And I recalled especially one game where Father Jack Daly stole home in the last of the ninth to put us ahead of our second-year juniors 1 to 0. Durocher would have hid under a bench in *that* rhubarb. Of course, monks had their own rhubarb vocabulary which, though violent at times, was usually distinctive as well. A certain umpire, for instance, was known for many years as "the good thief," not an unflattering title from the spiritual viewpoint, but not too heartwarming to an umpire.

The cemetery, too, was different. For one thing, part of it was in a different place. But the main difference was that these were no longer strangers who were buried here, but friends. They were not just the very old but also the very young. When we had first lived at Florissant as novices, the names on the headstones had been completely unfamiliar to us. But along the line of seventeen years, the Lord had taken home a lot of our friends. There was John Schenk who had died of leukemia in his second year of theology. There was Father Bob Huber who had drowned at Waupaca, Wisconsin, two weeks after his ordination. There was Father Frank Tully who had been brought home from Belize to die of cancer at the age of thirty-nine. There was Father Kleist, whom we had known so well; and Father Case, Father Mathery, and Father Thurb Smith.

At night, I looked out over the valley toward the highway and watched the cars going by with their bright lights and their promise, somehow, of pleasure, wealth, and honor, or just plain pleasure. And I remembered how, as a novice, I had sometimes thought that that was more the life for me than the life of prayer and work and sacrifice. But as I looked out this time, though I had had those lights in my eyes, or perhaps *because* they had flashed in my eyes, I had no more desire to travel that road, but only the overwhelming wish to serve God and to do something, some small, insignificant thing, to advance His Kingdom before this life should be all over. And it dawned on me that up to now, having only finished the Jesuit course a short time ago, I had given absolutely nothing but had received everything. And so, by looking at the lights of the world on the highway, I wanted to give every bit of my world back to God.

There are some new buildings which grace the grounds at Florissant and some new touches to the old buildings, but the place still looks the same. The new Juniorate

and new Novitiate stand out because it was in the old
Novitiate and old Juniorate that we spent most of our
time. It is good to see the new buildings. It's good to
realize that the old shoe rooms for instance, from the
old Juniorate and old Novitiate are things of the past.
It was in these rooms that Isaac's words to Jacob might
well have occurred to one: *Ecce odor filii mei sicut odor
agri pleni. . . .** But still, I missed the old buildings, probably because they had been old buildings.

The Rock Building, over one hundred years old, still
stands and looks like it will go on standing for another
hundred years. Here, we had first entered the Society.
Here we had first met those who were to be our companions for so many years. I can remember shaking
hands especially with Father Ben Schulte who really did
seem at the time to be loaded with dignity, but who
turned out to be a wonderful guy.

The Tertian Building, too, still stands and keeps its
unsuitable name — The Tertian Building.** The first
floor of this building is still the infirmary, now presided
over by Brother Mike Daniels.

The building in which we had lived as juniors now
houses the brothers. As I was walking outside this building one night during my visit, I remembered Father
Jacobsmeyer's history classes that had been held in the
corner recreation room, classes that we had enjoyed to a
man. It seemed only yesterday that we had sat there. I

---

* "Behold the odor of my son is like the odor of a full field"
(Gen. 27:27).
** Here, at one time, the Tertian Fathers of the Society
had lived during their third probation.

remembered the dormitory on the third floor, the first- and second-floor ascetories (rooms in which we all studied and had class). And I recalled particularly a speech class in which Father Budzinski had tried to get us all laughing to exercise the proper form of breathing. No one had been able to laugh, until Father John Wiggins had saved the day with a titter that resembled nothing so much as a wayward sneeze. The difficulty, then, was in getting us to stop laughing. For some reason or other we never tried that particular exercise again.

I recalled the old splash room in the basement of the Juniorate, where one of my contemporaries had spent so much time fashioning fishing plugs. These plugs he later tried out on the river, with the same result each and every time. His line always broke on the first attempt and he went back, resignedly enough, to manufacture another plug.

In the infirmary, the same small attractive chapel remains unchanged, except for a coat of paint. The little figures of our Lady and of the Infant Jesus above the altar are as charming, I think, as any I have seen. The Madonna is seated and the Infant stands with one foot on her lap while she obviously is tickling the other foot. Neither one, however, seems to be getting the proper kick out of it.

Back of the Novitiate and near the road, the dairy still functions. I noticed it especially because it was here that I worked each year on the feast of St. Alphonsus, when we scholastics used to take over for the brothers. Here we would wait until Father Urban Kramer brought in the milk from the farm, reached out a hand holding a can of milk as if it weighed only a pound at most, and told us to get to work. Then we would separate the milk, clean the cans and separator, and usually get pretty well singed with steam in the process.

The refectory looks just exactly as it did in our day, except that the pulpit is no longer there. In this modern age, the reader does his job from the side with the aid of a public-address system. In the refectory on some days when the juniors were giving sermons, I was happy to notice that their attitude toward the whole brutal business was much the same as ours had been. The first junior to give a sermon, during the time of my visit, looked just as grim as I had always felt before mine. He gradually got into his sermon and even semed to enjoy it somewhat. But he couldn't help the tremendous smile of relief that went from ear to ear when he had finished — his own ears as well as those of his audience. One day they read from the Menology* of the Missouri Province about some supposedly holy Missouri Jesuit who was described as "hard on himself" (which is perfectly all right) and it was inferred that he was "equally hard on others . . ." I couldn't help wondering if the author of that Menology had considered the latter characteristic a virtue. Fortunately, I have met very few in the Society who do.

The meals, on my visit, were as wonderful as they were big and certainly did not justify the question that I had so often asked Brother Schwendemann: "What, pork again?" Even if we happened to have steak or chicken I

---

* The Menology is a collection of edifying incidents in the lives of local Jesuits or even entire biographies of such men.

always asked this question and received an appropriate answer. I was a little disappointed the first few days of my visit that no corn bread — without which there would undoubtedly be much smaller Jesuits — was served. But I soon discovered my mistake. When it rains it pours. It came down one evening in the shape of pies, two nights later in squares, and two nights after that in muffin form. So I felt better. I was pleased, too, to find that the novices and juniors ate as much as ever, so that I did not have to finish my own meal in complete solitude.

There was one change in the refectory that was distracting. Someone along the line had invested in a great number of plastic dishes and, during Lent when there is no reading and all else is quiet, a community eating off these dishes sounds like a flock of gamecocks having it out in a rain trough.

Even though I am not any great spiritual man nor even the ordinary spiritual man I should be, I still consider the chapel at Florissant a favorite spot. Today, it sports a very beautiful new paint job, though I noticed that there is still trouble with crumbling plaster on the gospel side. Everything about the chapel is so familiar — the steps leading to its doors, up which I had made my way once, heroically as I thought, with a bad Charley horse. The act did not seem so heroic when I met the Master of Novices glaring at me from the top step.

Just outside the chapel is the picture of the *Ecce Homo* which I have always thought so much of, despite the fact that another novice told me it is very poor art. There too, in front of the chapel, are the statues of St. John Berchmans, patron of juniors, on the Juniorate side and of St. Stanislaus Kostka, patron of novices, on the Novitiate side. And above the entrance to the bridge going to the old Juniorate is the picture of the Immaculate Heart of Mary.

At the front of the chapel on either side are the statues of St. Ignatius and St. Francis Xavier. Xavier's arm, holding a crucifix, is still impossibly contorted, and there is still just the slightest evidence of the black spot on St. Ignatius' foot, which was caused by Brother Terry, who used to touch the foot of Ignatius with his hand and then kiss the hand. The Stations of the Cross, too, have a new coat of paint, but they are still the same.

I was glad to be in the chapel during Sunday Mass and Benediction, because on a much earlier visit it had been the singing of the novices and juniors which had first, crazily enough, made me begin to think of entering the Society. The singing was good now, but in our day we were much louder. Of course, we had voices then like that of Father Ed McCarthy, with enough power to liven things up.

I watched the novice sacristan at work and reflected that sacristans did not change, either. Nothing is superior to a sacristan. And even among this superior breed, Father Tim Cronin, who had been sacristan in our day, made the rest seem like the hired help bowing before the butler.

No, I'll never forget that chapel, because it was here I had first learned to know God a little. It was here all of us had asked God to make us love Him above all creatures. It was here we found the answers to our questions, answers that we could never find, or put, in books.

"I have finished the course."

Yes, it was good to get back for a time to the House of Bread. I hoped, on my visit that these men, youngsters as Jesuits go, would enjoy their whole course in the Society as much as I had, or, if that were possible, even more. I hoped that they, too, would realize what a privilege it is to be a Jesuit. I realize it because I know that I am and always have been unworthy of the company God has put me in.

Someday, I might die of some horrible disease that will make laughing a little bit difficult. But, even though I might not be able to laugh on the outside since I am and undoubtedly still will be a coward, inside I'll be thinking of the fun I've had, even in the midst of some heartaches involved in trying in my stumbling way to serve God. And I'll know that there's even more fun ahead because He's promised us a hundredfold. So, even if it kills me, I'll die laughing!